WHO FRAMEWORK CONVENTION ON TOBACCO CONTROL

Guidelines
for implementation

Article 5.3 | Article 8 | Articles 9 and 10
Article 11 | Article 12 | Article 13 | Article 14

2013
edition

WHO Library Cataloguing-in-Publication Data :

WHO Framework Convention on Tobacco Control: guidelines for implementation
Article 5.3; Article 8; Articles 9 and 10; Article 11; Article 12; Article 13; Article 14 –
2013 edition.

1.Tobacco industry - legislation. 2.Smoking - adverse effects. 3.Smoking - legislation. 4.Tobacco-derived products labelling. 5.Tobacco control campaigns. I.World Health Organization.

ISBN 978 92 4 150518 5   (NLM classification: HD 9130.6)

© **World Health Organization 2013**

All rights reserved. Publications of the World Health Organization are available on the WHO web site (www.who.int) or can be purchased from WHO Press, World Health Organization, 20 Avenue Appia, 1211 Geneva 27, Switzerland (tel.: +41 22 791 3264; fax: +41 22 791 4857; e-mail: bookorders@who.int).

Requests for permission to reproduce or translate WHO publications – whether for sale or for non-commercial distribution – should be addressed to WHO Press through the WHO web site (www.who.int/about/licensing/copyright_form/en/index.html).
The designations employed and the presentation of the material in this publication do not imply the expression of any opinion whatsoever on the part of the World Health Organization concerning the legal status of any country, territory, city or area or of its authorities, or concerning the delimitation of its frontiers or boundaries. Dotted lines on maps represent approximate border lines for which there may not yet be full agreement.

The mention of specific companies or of certain manufacturers' products does not imply that they are endorsed or recommended by the World Health Organization in preference to others of a similar nature that are not mentioned. Errors and omissions excepted, the names of proprietary products are distinguished by initial capital letters.

All reasonable precautions have been taken by the World Health Organization to verify the information contained in this publication. However, the published material is being distributed without warranty of any kind, either expressed or implied. The responsibility for the interpretation and use of the material lies with the reader. In no event shall the World Health Organization be liable for damages arising from its use.

Printed in France

TABLE OF CONTENTS

GUIDELINES FOR IMPLEMENTATION OF ARTICLE 5.3
OF THE WHO FRAMEWORK CONVENTION ON TOBACCO CONTROL
Protection of public health policies with respect to tobacco control
from commercial and other vested interests of the tobacco industry 1

GUIDELINES FOR IMPLEMENTATION OF ARTICLE 8
OF THE WHO FRAMEWORK CONVENTION ON TOBACCO CONTROL
Protection from exposure to tobacco smoke 17

PARTIAL GUIDELINES FOR IMPLEMENTATION OF ARTICLES 9 AND 10
OF THE WHO FRAMEWORK CONVENTION ON TOBACCO CONTROL
Regulation of the contents of tobacco products
and of tobacco product disclosures 31

GUIDELINES FOR IMPLEMENTATION OF ARTICLE 11
OF THE WHO FRAMEWORK CONVENTION ON TOBACCO CONTROL
Packaging and labelling of tobacco products 53

GUIDELINES FOR IMPLEMENTATION OF ARTICLE 12
OF THE WHO FRAMEWORK CONVENTION ON TOBACCO CONTROL
Education, communication, training and public awareness 71

GUIDELINES FOR IMPLEMENTATION OF ARTICLE 13
OF THE WHO FRAMEWORK CONVENTION ON TOBACCO CONTROL
Tobacco advertising, promotion and sponsorship 93

GUIDELINES FOR IMPLEMENTATION OF ARTICLE 14
OF THE WHO FRAMEWORK CONVENTION ON TOBACCO CONTROL
Demand reduction measures concerning tobacco
dependence and cessation 115

FOREWORD

This publication contains the guidelines adopted by the Conference of the Parties (COP) to the WHO Framework Convention on Tobacco Control (WHO FCTC) at its second (2007), third (2008), fourth (2010) and fifth (2012) sessions. It has been prepared by the Convention Secretariat in order to promote implementation of the Convention. The first (2011) edition of the guidelines was published following the fourth session of the COP. This 2013 edition takes into account the amendments made to the partial guidelines for implementation of Articles 9 and 10 of the WHO FCTC adopted by the COP at its fifth session.

The seven guidelines cover a wide range of provisions of the WHO FCTC, such as:

- protection of public health policies with respect to tobacco control from commercial and other vested interests of the tobacco industry (Article 5.3);
- protection from exposure to tobacco smoke (Article 8);
- regulation of the contents of tobacco products and of tobacco product disclosures (Articles 9 and 10);
- packaging and labelling of tobacco products (Article 11);
- education, communication, training and public awareness (Article 12);
- tobacco advertising, promotion and sponsorship (Article 13); and
- demand reduction measures concerning tobacco dependence and cessation (Article 14).

The guidelines are intended to help Parties to meet their obligations under the respective provisions of the Convention. They reflect the consolidated views of Parties on different aspects of implementation, their experiences and achievements, and the challenges faced. The guidelines also aim to reflect and promote best practices and standards that governments would benefit from in the treaty-implementation process.

The guidelines were prepared through the work of representatives of the Parties in the intergovernmental working groups established by the Conference of the Parties, intergovernmental and nongovernmental organizations accredited as observers to the COP and invited experts, with further input from Parties during the commentary process and the discussions during sessions of the COP.

As a result of this wide consultative process and the consensus reached by the Parties, the guidelines have become widely acknowledged as a valuable tool in the implementation of the Convention.

Dr Haik Nikogosian
Head of the Convention Secretariat

Guidelines for implementation
Article 5.3

Guidelines for implementation of Article 5.3 of the WHO Framework Convention on Tobacco Control

PROTECTION OF PUBLIC HEALTH POLICIES WITH RESPECT TO TOBACCO CONTROL FROM COMMERCIAL AND OTHER VESTED INTERESTS OF THE TOBACCO INDUSTRY

INTRODUCTION

World Health Assembly resolution WHA54.18 on transparency in tobacco control process, citing the findings of the Committee of Experts on Tobacco Industry Documents, states that "the tobacco industry has operated for years with the express intention of subverting the role of governments and of WHO in implementing public health policies to combat the tobacco epidemic".

The Preamble of the WHO Framework Convention on Tobacco Control recognized the Parties'[1] "need to be alert to any efforts by the tobacco industry to undermine or subvert tobacco control efforts and the need to be informed of activities of the tobacco industry that have a negative impact on tobacco control efforts".

Further, Article 5.3 of the Convention requires that "in setting and implementing their public health policies with respect to tobacco control, Parties shall act to protect these policies from commercial and other vested interests of the tobacco industry in accordance with national law".

The Conference of the Parties, in decision FCTC/COP2(14), established a working group to elaborate guidelines for implementation of Article 5.3 of the Convention.

Without prejudice to the sovereign right of the Parties to determine and establish their tobacco control policies, Parties are encouraged to implement these guidelines to the extent possible in accordance with their national law.

Purpose, scope and applicability

Use of the guidelines for implementation of Article 5.3 of the Convention will have an overarching impact on countries' tobacco control policies and on implementation of the Convention, because the guidelines recognize that

---

[1] "The term 'Parties' refers to States and other entities with treaty-making capacity which have expressed their consent to be bound by a treaty and where the treaty is in force for such States and entities." (Source: United Nations Treaty Collections: http://untreaty.un.org/English/guide.asp#signatories).

tobacco industry interference, including that from the State-owned tobacco industry, cuts across a number of tobacco control policy areas, as stated in the Preamble of the Convention, articles referring to specific tobacco control policies and the Rules of Procedure of the Conference of the Parties to the WHO Framework Convention on Tobacco Control.

The purpose of these guidelines is to ensure that efforts to protect tobacco control from commercial and other vested interests of the tobacco industry are comprehensive and effective. Parties should implement measures in all branches of government that may have an interest in, or the capacity to, affect public health policies with respect to tobacco control.

The aim of these guidelines is to assist Parties[2] in meeting their legal obligations under Article 5.3 of the Convention. The guidelines draw on the best available scientific evidence and the experience of Parties in addressing tobacco industry interference.

The guidelines apply to setting and implementing Parties' public health policies with respect to tobacco control. They also apply to persons, bodies or entities that contribute to, or could contribute to, the formulation, implementation, administration or enforcement of those policies.

The guidelines are applicable to government officials, representatives and employees of any national, state, provincial, municipal, local or other public or semi/quasi-public institution or body within the jurisdiction of a Party, and to any person acting on their behalf. Any government branch (executive, legislative and judiciary) responsible for setting and implementing tobacco control policies and for protecting those policies against tobacco industry interests should be accountable.

The broad array of strategies and tactics used by the tobacco industry to interfere with the setting and implementing of tobacco control measures, such as those that Parties to the Convention are required to implement, is documented by a vast body of evidence. The measures recommended in these guidelines aim at protecting against interference not only by the tobacco industry but also, as appropriate, by organizations and individuals that work to further the interests of the tobacco industry.

While the measures recommended in these guidelines should be applied by Parties as broadly as necessary, in order best to achieve the objectives of Article 5.3 of the Convention, Parties are strongly urged to implement measures beyond those recommended in these guidelines when adapting them to their specific circumstances.

---

[2] Where appropriate, these guidelines also refer to regional economic integration organizations.

GUIDING PRINCIPLES

Principle 1: There is a fundamental and irreconcilable conflict between the tobacco industry's interests and public health policy interests.

The tobacco industry produces and promotes a product that has been proven scientifically to be addictive, to cause disease and death and to give rise to a variety of social ills, including increased poverty. Therefore, Parties should protect the formulation and implementation of public health policies for tobacco control from the tobacco industry to the greatest extent possible.

Principle 2: Parties, when dealing with the tobacco industry or those working to further its interests, should be accountable and transparent.

Parties should ensure that any interaction with the tobacco industry on matters related to tobacco control or public health is accountable and transparent.

Principle 3: Parties should require the tobacco industry and those working to further its interests to operate and act in a manner that is accountable and transparent.

The tobacco industry should be required to provide Parties with information for effective implementation of these guidelines.

Principle 4: Because their products are lethal, the tobacco industry should not be granted incentives to establish or run their businesses.

Any preferential treatment of the tobacco industry would be in conflict with tobacco control policy.

RECOMMENDATIONS

The following important activities are recommended for addressing tobacco industry interference in public health policies:

(1) Raise awareness about the addictive and harmful nature of tobacco products and about tobacco industry interference with Parties' tobacco control policies.

(2) Establish measures to limit interactions with the tobacco industry and ensure the transparency of those interactions that occur.

(3) Reject partnerships and non-binding or non-enforceable agreements with the tobacco industry.

(4) Avoid conflicts of interest for government officials and employees.

(5) Require that information provided by the tobacco industry be transparent and accurate

(6) Denormalize and, to the extent possible, regulate activities described as "socially responsible" by the tobacco industry, including but not limited to activities described as "corporate social responsibility".

(7) Do not give preferential treatment to the tobacco industry.

(8) Treat State-owned tobacco industry in the same way as any other tobacco industry.

Agreed measures for protecting public health policies with respect to tobacco control from commercial and other vested interests of the tobacco industry are listed below. Parties are encouraged to implement measures beyond those provided for by these guidelines, and nothing in these guidelines shall prevent a Party from imposing stricter requirements that are consistent with these recommendations.

(1) Raise awareness about the addictive and harmful nature of tobacco products and about tobacco industry interference with Parties' tobacco control policies.

All branches of government and the public need knowledge and awareness about past and present interference by the tobacco industry in setting and implementing public health policies with respect to tobacco control. Such interference requires specific action for successful implementation of the whole Framework Convention.

Recommendations

1.1 Parties should, in consideration of Article 12 of the Convention, inform and educate all branches of government and the public about the addictive and harmful nature of tobacco products, the need to protect public health policies for tobacco control from commercial and other vested interests of the tobacco industry and the strategies and tactics used by the tobacco industry to interfere with the setting and implementation of public health policies with respect to tobacco control.

1.2 Parties should, in addition, raise awareness about the tobacco industry's practice of using individuals, front groups and affiliated organizations to act, openly or covertly, on their behalf or to take action to further the interests of the tobacco industry.

(2) Establish measures to limit interactions with the tobacco industry and ensure the transparency of those interactions that occur.

In setting and implementing public health policies with respect to tobacco control, any necessary interaction with the tobacco industry should be carried out by Parties in such a way as to avoid the creation of any perception of a real or potential partnership or cooperation resulting from or on account of such interaction. In the event the tobacco industry engages in any conduct that may create such a perception, Parties should act to prevent or correct this perception.

Recommendations

2.1 Parties should interact with the tobacco industry only when and to the extent strictly necessary to enable them to effectively regulate the tobacco industry and tobacco products.

2.2 Where interactions with the tobacco industry are necessary, Parties should ensure that such interactions are conducted transparently. Whenever possible, interactions should be conducted in public, for example through public hearings, public notice of interactions, disclosure of records of such interactions to the public.

(3) Reject partnerships and non-binding or non-enforceable agreements with the tobacco industry.

The tobacco industry should not be a partner in any initiative linked to setting or implementing public health policies, given that its interests are in direct conflict with the goals of public health.

Recommendations

3.1 Parties should not accept, support or endorse partnerships and non-binding or non-enforceable agreements as well as any voluntary arrangement with the tobacco industry or any entity or person working to further its interests.

3.2 Parties should not accept, support or endorse the tobacco industry organizing, promoting, participating in, or performing, youth, public education or any initiatives that are directly or indirectly related to tobacco control.

3.3 Parties should not accept, support or endorse any voluntary code of conduct or instrument drafted by the tobacco industry that is offered as a substitute for legally enforceable tobacco control measures.

3.4 Parties should not accept, support or endorse any offer for assistance or proposed tobacco control legislation or policy drafted by or in collaboration with the tobacco industry.

(4) Avoid conflicts of interest for government officials and employees.

The involvement of organizations or individuals with commercial or vested interests in the tobacco industry in public health policies with respect to tobacco control is most likely to have a negative effect. Clear rules regarding conflicts of interest for government officials and employees working in tobacco control are important means for protecting such policies from interference by the tobacco industry.

Payments, gifts and services, monetary or in-kind, and research funding offered by the tobacco industry to government institutions, officials or employees can create conflicts of interest. Conflicting interests are created even if a promise of favourable consideration is not given in exchange, as the potential exists for personal interest to influence official responsibilities as recognized in the International Code of Conduct for Public Officials adopted by the United Nations General Assembly and by several governmental and regional economic integration organizations.

Recommendations

4.1 Parties should mandate a policy on the disclosure and management of conflicts of interest that applies to all persons involved in setting and implementing public health policies with respect to tobacco control, including government officials, employees, consultants and contractors.

4.2 Parties should formulate, adopt and implement a code of conduct for public officials, prescribing the standards with which they should comply in their dealings with the tobacco industry.

4.3 Parties should not award contracts for carrying out any work related to setting and implementing public health policies with respect to tobacco control to candidates or tenderers who have conflicts of interest with established tobacco control policies.

4.4 Parties should develop clear policies that require public office holders who have or have had a role in setting and implementing public health policies with respect to tobacco control to inform their institutions about any intention to engage in an occupational activity within the tobacco industry, whether gainful or not, within a specified period of time after leaving service.

4.5 Parties should develop clear policies that require applicants for public office positions which have a role in setting and implementing public health policies with respect to tobacco control to declare any current or previous occupational activity with any tobacco industry whether gainful or not.

4.6 Parties should require government officials to declare and divest themselves of direct interests in the tobacco industry.

4.7 Government institutions and their bodies should not have any financial interest in the tobacco industry, unless they are responsible for managing a Party's ownership interest in a State-owned tobacco industry.

4.8 Parties should not allow any person employed by the tobacco industry or any entity working to further its interests to be a member of any government body, committee or advisory group that sets or implements tobacco control or public health policy.

4.9 Parties should not nominate any person employed by the tobacco industry or any entity working to further its interests to serve on delegations to meetings of the Conference of the Parties, its subsidiary bodies or any other bodies established pursuant to decisions of the Conference of the Parties.

4.10 Parties should not allow any official or employee of government or of any semi/quasi-governmental body to accept payments, gifts or services, monetary or in-kind, from the tobacco industry.

4.11 Taking into account national law and constitutional principles, Parties should have effective measures to prohibit contributions from the tobacco industry or any entity working to further its interests to political parties, candidates or campaigns, or to require full disclosure of such contributions.

(5) Require that information provided by the tobacco industry be transparent and accurate.

To take effective measures preventing interference of the tobacco industry with public health policies, Parties need information about its activities and practices, thus ensuring that the industry operates in a transparent manner. Article 12 of the Convention requires Parties to promote public access to such information in accordance with national law.

Article 20.4 of the Convention requires, inter alia, Parties to promote and facilitate exchanges of information about tobacco industry practices and the cultivation of tobacco. In accordance with Article 20.4(c) of the Convention, each Party should endeavour to cooperate with competent international organizations to establish progressively and maintain a global system to regularly collect and disseminate information on tobacco production and manufacture and activities of the tobacco industry which have an impact on the Convention or national tobacco control activities.

Recommendations

5.1 Parties should introduce and apply measures to ensure that all operations and activities of the tobacco industry are transparent.[3]

5.2 Parties should require the tobacco industry and those working to further its interests to periodically submit information on tobacco production, manufacture, market share, marketing expenditures, revenues and any other activity, including lobbying, philanthropy, political contributions and all other activities not prohibited or not yet prohibited under Article 13 of the Convention.[3]

5.3 Parties should require rules for the disclosure or registration of the tobacco industry entities, affiliated organizations and individuals acting on their behalf, including lobbyists.

5.4 Parties should impose mandatory penalties on the tobacco industry in case of the provision of false or misleading information in accordance with national law.

5.5 Parties should adopt and implement effective legislative, executive, administrative and other measures to ensure public access, in accordance with Article 12(c) of the Convention, to a wide range of information on tobacco industry activities as relevant to the objectives of the Convention, such as in a public repository.

(6) Denormalize and, to the extent possible, regulate activities described as "socially responsible" by the tobacco industry, including but not limited to activities described as "corporate social responsibility".

The tobacco industry conducts activities described as socially responsible to distance its image from the lethal nature of the product it produces and sells or to interfere with the setting and implementation of public health policies. Activities that are described as "socially responsible" by the tobacco industry, aiming at the promotion of tobacco consumption, is a marketing as well as a public relations strategy that falls within the Convention's definition of advertising, promotion and sponsorship.

The corporate social responsibility of the tobacco industry is, according to WHO,[4] an inherent contradiction, as industry's core functions are in conflict with the goals of public health policies with respect to tobacco control.

Recommendations

6.1 Parties should ensure that all branches of government and the public are informed and made aware of the true purpose and

---

[3] Without prejudice to trade secrets or confidential information protected by law.

[4] WHO. *Tobacco industry and corporate social responsibility – an inherent contradiction*. Geneva, World Health Organization, 2004.

scope of activities described as socially responsible performed by the tobacco industry.

6.2 Parties should not endorse, support, form partnerships with or participate in activities of the tobacco industry described as socially responsible.

6.3 Parties should not allow public disclosure by the tobacco industry or any other person acting on its behalf of activities described as socially responsible or of the expenditures made for these activities, except when legally required to report on such expenditures, such as in an annual report.[5]

6.4 Parties should not allow acceptance by any branch of government or the public sector of political, social, financial, educational, community or other contributions from the tobacco industry or from those working to further its interests, except for compensations due to legal settlements or mandated by law or legally binding and enforceable agreements.

(7) Do not give preferential treatment to the tobacco industry.

Some governments encourage investments by the tobacco industry, even to the extent of subsidizing them with financial incentives, such as providing partial or complete exemption from taxes otherwise mandated by law.

Without prejudice to their sovereign right to determine and establish their economic, financial and taxation policies, Parties should respect their commitments for tobacco control.

Recommendations

7.1 Parties should not grant incentives, privileges or benefits to the tobacco industry to establish or run their businesses.

7.2 Parties that do not have a State-owned tobacco industry should not invest in the tobacco industry and related ventures. Parties with a State-owned tobacco industry should ensure that any investment in the tobacco industry does not prevent them from fully implementing the WHO Framework Convention on Tobacco Control.

7.3 Parties should not provide any preferential tax exemption to the tobacco industry.

---

[5] The guidelines for implementation of Article 13 of the WHO Framework Convention on Tobacco Control address this subject from the perspective of tobacco advertising, promotion and sponsorship.

(8) Treat State-owned tobacco industry in the same way as any other tobacco industry.

Tobacco industry can be government-owned, non-government-owned or a combination thereof. These guidelines apply to all tobacco industry, regardless of its ownership.

Recommendations

8.1 Parties should ensure that State-owned tobacco industry is treated in the same way as any other member of the tobacco industry in respect of setting and implementing tobacco control policy.

8.2 Parties should ensure that the setting and implementing of tobacco control policy are separated from overseeing or managing tobacco industry.

8.3 Parties should ensure that representatives of State-owned tobacco industry does not form part of delegations to any meetings of the Conference of the Parties, its subsidiary bodies or any other bodies established pursuant to decisions of the Conference of the Parties.

ENFORCEMENT AND MONITORING

Enforcement

Parties should put in place enforcement mechanisms or, to the extent possible, use existing enforcement mechanisms to meet their obligations under Article 5.3 of the Convention and these guidelines.

Monitoring implementation of Article 5.3 of the Convention and of these guidelines

Monitoring implementation of Article 5.3 of the Convention and of these guidelines is essential for ensuring the introduction and implementation of efficient tobacco control policies. This should also involve monitoring the tobacco industry, for which existing models and resources should be used, such as the database on tobacco industry monitoring of the WHO Tobacco Free Initiative.

Nongovernmental organizations and other members of civil society not affiliated with the tobacco industry could play an essential role in monitoring the activities of the tobacco industry.

Codes of conduct or staff regulations for all branches of governments should include a "whistleblower function", with adequate protection of whistleblowers.

In addition, Parties should be encouraged to use and enforce mechanisms to ensure compliance with these guidelines, such as the possibility of bringing an action to court, and to use complaint procedures such as an ombudsman system.

INTERNATIONAL COLLABORATION AND UPDATING AND REVISION OF THE GUIDELINES

International cooperation is essential for making progress in preventing interference by the tobacco industry with the formulation of public health policies on tobacco control. Article 20.4 of the Convention provides the basis for collecting and exchanging knowledge and experience with respect to tobacco industry practices, taking into account and addressing the special needs of developing country Parties and Parties with economies in transition.

Efforts have already been made to coordinate the collection and dissemination of national and international experience with regard to the strategies and tactics used by the tobacco industry and to the monitoring of tobacco industry activities. Parties would benefit from sharing legal and strategic expertise for countering tobacco industry strategies. Article 21.4 of the Convention provides that information exchange should be subject to national laws regarding confidentiality and privacy.

Recommendations

As the strategies and tactics used by the tobacco industry evolve constantly, these guidelines should be reviewed and revised periodically to ensure that they continue to provide effective guidance to Parties on protecting their public health policies on tobacco control from tobacco industry interference.

Parties reporting via the existing reporting instrument of the Framework Convention should provide information on tobacco production and manufacture and the activities of the tobacco industry that affect the Convention or national tobacco control activities. To facilitate this exchange, the Convention Secretariat should ensure that the principal provisions of these guidelines are reflected in the next phases of the reporting instrument, which the Conference of the Parties will gradually adopt for use by Parties.

In view of the paramount importance of preventing tobacco industry interference in any public health policy with respect to tobacco control, the Conference of the Parties may, in the light of experience with implementing these guidelines, consider whether there is a need to elaborate a protocol in relation to Article 5.3 of the Convention.

USEFUL SOURCES OF INFORMATION

Relevant literature

Brandt AM. *The cigarette century. The rise, fall, and deadly persistence of the product that defined America*. New York, Basic Books, 2007.

Chapman S. *Making smoking history. Public health advocacy and tobacco control*. Oxford, Blackwell Publishing, 2007.

Callard C, Thompson D, Collishaw N. *Curing the addiction to profits: a supply-side approach to phasing out tobacco*. Ottawa, Canadian Centre for Policy Alternatives and Physicians for a Smoke free Canada, 2005.

Feldman EA, Bayer R (Editors). *Unfiltered: conflicts over tobacco policy and public health*. Boston, Harvard University Press, 2004.

Gilmore A et al. Continuing influence of tobacco industry in Germany. *Lancet*, 2002, 360:1255.

Hastings G, Angus K. *The influence of the tobacco industry on European tobacco control policy. In: Tobacco or health in the European Union. Past, present and future*. Luxembourg, Office for Official Publications of the European Commission, 2004:195–225.

Lavack A. *Tobacco industry denormalization campaigns: a review and evaluation*. Ottawa, Health Canada, 2001.

Mahood G. *Tobacco industry denormalization. Telling the truth about the tobacco industry's role in the tobacco epidemic*. Toronto, Campaign for Tobacco Industry Denormalization, 2004.

Pan American Health Organization. *Profits over people. Tobacco industry activities to market cigarettes and undermine public health in Latin America and the Caribbean*. Washington DC, Pan American Health Organization, 2002.

Simpson D. Germany: still sleeping with the enemy. *Tobacco Control*, 2003, 12:343–344.

Hammond R, Rowell A. *Trust us. We're the tobacco industry*. Baltimore, Johns Hopkins University Press, 2001.

World Health Organization. *Tobacco company strategies to undermine tobacco control activities at the World Health Organization*. Geneva, World Health Organization, 2000.

World Health Organization. *Tobacco industry and corporate social responsibility – an inherent contradiction*. Geneva, World Health Organization, 2004.

Yach D, Bialous S. Junking science to promote tobacco. *American Journal of Public Health*, 2001, 91:1745–1748.

Web resources

WHO sites:
Tobacco Free Initiative: http://www.who.int/tobacco/en/

WHO publications on tobacco:
http://www.who.int/tobacco/resources/publications/en/

WHO European Regional Office:
http://www.euro.who.int/healthtopics/HT2ndLvlPage?HTCode=smoking

Tobacco control in the Americas (in English and Spanish):
http://www.paho.org/english/ad/sde/ra/Tobabout.htm

Sites with general, regional or national information and topics related to tobacco control:
Action on Smoking and Health, UK (and special page for the tobacco industry):
http://www.newash.org.uk/ash_r3iitasl.htm

Corporate Accountability International and the Network for Accountability of Tobacco Transnationals: www.stopcorporateabuse.org

Economics of tobacco control: http://www1.worldbank.org/tobacco/

European Commission:
http://ec.europa.eu/health/ph_determinants/life_style/Tobacco/tobacco_en.htm

European Network for Smoking Prevention: http://www.ensp.org/

Framework Convention Alliance for Tobacco Control: http://www.fctc.org/

International Union for Health Promotion and Education:
http://www.iuhpe.org/?page=18&lang=en

Model Legislation for Tobacco Control manual:
http://www.iuhpe.org/?lang=en&page=publications_report2

Tobacco industry:
http://tobacco.health.usyd.edu.au/site/supersite/links/docs/tobacco_ind.htm

Smokefree Partnership: http://www.smokefreepartnership.eu/

Thailand Health Promotion Institute: http://www.thpinhf.org/

Tobaccopedia: the online tobacco encyclopaedia: http://www.tobaccopedia.org/

More links to tobacco sites:

Various international and national tobacco control web sites:
http://www.tobacco.org/resources/general/tobsites.html

National tobacco control web sites:
http://www.smokefreepartnership.eu/National-Tobacco-Control-websites

Centre de ressources anti-tabac: http://www.tabac-info.net/

Comité National Contre le Tabagisme (France): http://www.cnct.org

Office Français de Prévention du Tabagisme: http://www.oft-asso.fr/

Latest news on smoking and tobacco control: http://www.globalink.org

Ministère de la santé, de la jeunesse et des sports: http://www.sante.gouv.fr/

Guidelines for implementation
Article 8

Guidelines for implementation of Article 8 of the WHO Framework Convention on Tobacco Control

PROTECTION FROM EXPOSURE TO TOBACCO SMOKE

PURPOSE, OBJECTIVES AND KEY CONSIDERATIONS

Purpose of the guidelines

Consistent with other provisions of the WHO FCTC and the intentions of the Conference of the Parties, these guidelines are intended to assist Parties in meeting their obligations under Article 8 of the Convention. They draw on the best available evidence and the experience of Parties that have successfully implemented effective measures to reduce exposure to tobacco smoke.

The guidelines contain agreed upon statements of principles and definitions of relevant terms, as well as agreed upon recommendations for the steps required to satisfy the obligations of the Convention. In addition, the guidelines identify the measures necessary to achieve effective protection from the hazards of second-hand tobacco smoke. Parties are encouraged to use these guidelines not only to fulfil their legal duties under the Convention, but also to follow best practices in protecting public health.

Objectives of the guidelines

These guidelines have two related objectives. The first is to assist Parties in meeting their obligations under Article 8 of the WHO FCTC, in a manner consistent with the scientific evidence regarding exposure to second-hand tobacco smoke and the best practice worldwide in the implementation of smoke free measures, in order to establish a high standard of accountability for treaty compliance and to assist the Parties in promoting the highest attainable standard of health. The second objective is to identify the key elements of legislation necessary to effectively protect people from exposure to tobacco smoke, as required by Article 8.

Underlying considerations

The development of these guidelines has been influenced by the following fundamental considerations.

(a) The duty to protect from tobacco smoke, embodied in the text of Article 8, is grounded in fundamental human rights and freedoms. Given the dangers of breathing second-hand tobacco smoke, the duty to protect from tobacco smoke is implicit in, inter alia, the right to life and the right to the highest attainable standard of health, as recognized in many international legal instruments (including the Constitution of the World Health Organization, the Convention on the Rights of the Child, the Convention on the Elimination of all Forms of Discrimination against Women and the Covenant on Economic, Social and Cultural Rights), as formally incorporated into the preamble of the WHO FCTC and as recognized in the constitutions of many nations.

(b) The duty to protect individuals from tobacco smoke corresponds to an obligation by governments to enact legislation to protect individuals against threats to their fundamental rights and freedoms. This obligation extends to all persons, and not merely to certain populations.

(c) Several authoritative scientific bodies have determined that second-hand tobacco smoke is a carcinogen. Some Parties to the WHO FCTC (for example, Finland and Germany have classified second-hand tobacco smoke as a carcinogen and included the prevention of exposure to it at work in their health and safety legislation. In addition to the requirements of Article 8, therefore, Parties may be obligated to address the hazard of exposure to tobacco smoke in accordance with their existing workplace laws or other laws governing exposure to harmful substances, including carcinogens.

STATEMENT OF PRINCIPLES AND RELEVANT DEFINITIONS UNDERLYING PROTECTION FROM EXPOSURE TO TOBACCO SMOKE

Principles

As noted in Article 4 of the WHO FCTC, strong political commitment is necessary to take measures to protect all persons from exposure to tobacco smoke. The following agreed upon principles should guide the implementation of Article 8 of the Convention.

Principle 1

Effective measures to provide protection from exposure to tobacco smoke, as envisioned by Article 8 of the WHO FCTC, require the total elimination of smoking and tobacco smoke in a particular space or environment in order to create a 100% smoke free environment. There is no safe level of exposure to tobacco smoke, and notions such as a threshold value for toxicity from second-hand smoke should be rejected, as they are contradicted by scientific evidence. Approaches other than 100% smoke free environments, including ventilation, air filtration and the use of designated smoking areas (whether with separate ventilation systems or not), have repeatedly been shown to be ineffective and there is conclusive evidence, scientific and otherwise, that engineering approaches do not protect against exposure to tobacco smoke.

Principle 2
> All people should be protected from exposure to tobacco smoke. All indoor workplaces and indoor public places should be smoke free.

Principle 3
> Legislation is necessary to protect people from exposure to tobacco smoke. Voluntary smoke free policies have repeatedly been shown to be ineffective and do not provide adequate protection. In order to be effective, legislation should be simple, clear and enforceable.

Principle 4
> Good planning and adequate resources are essential for successful implementation and enforcement of smoke free legislation.

Principle 5
> Civil society has a central role in building support for and ensuring compliance with smoke free measures, and should be included as an active partner in the process of developing, implementing and enforcing legislation.

Principle 6
> The implementation of smoke free legislation, its enforcement and its impact should all be monitored and evaluated. This should include monitoring and responding to tobacco industry activities that undermine the implementation and enforcement of the legislation, as specified in Article 20.4 of the WHO FCTC.

Principle 7
> The protection of people from exposure to tobacco smoke should be strengthened and expanded, if necessary; such action may include new or amended legislation, improved enforcement and other measures to reflect new scientific evidence and case-study experiences.

Definitions

In developing legislation, it is important to use care in defining key terms. Several recommendations as to appropriate definitions, based on experiences in many countries, are set out here. The definitions in this section supplement those already included in the WHO FCTC.

"Second-hand tobacco smoke" or "environmental tobacco smoke"

Several alternative terms are commonly used to describe the type of smoke addressed by Article 8 of the WHO FCTC. These include "second-hand smoke", "environmental tobacco smoke", and "other people's smoke". Terms such as

Guidelines for implementation: Article 8

"passive smoking" and "involuntary exposure to tobacco smoke" should be avoided, as experience in France and elsewhere suggests that the tobacco industry may use these terms to support a position that "voluntary" exposure is acceptable. "Second hand tobacco smoke", sometimes abbreviated as "SHS", and "environmental tobacco smoke", sometimes abbreviated "ETS", are the preferable terms; these guidelines use "second-hand tobacco smoke".

Second-hand tobacco smoke can be defined as "the smoke emitted from the burning end of a cigarette or from other tobacco products usually in combination with the smoke exhaled by the smoker".

"Smoke free air" is air that is 100% smoke free. This definition includes, but is not limited to, air in which tobacco smoke cannot be seen, smelled, sensed or measured.[1]

"Smoking"
This term should be defined to include being in possession or control of a lit tobacco product regardless of whether the smoke is being actively inhaled or exhaled.

"Public places"
While the precise definition of "public places" will vary between jurisdictions, it is important that legislation define this term as broadly as possible. The definition used should cover all places accessible to the general public or places for collective use, regardless of ownership or right to access.

"Indoor" or "enclosed"
Article 8 requires protection from tobacco smoke in "indoor" workplaces and public places. Because there are potential pitfalls in defining "indoor" areas, the experiences of various countries in defining this term should be specifically examined. The definition should be as inclusive and as clear as possible, and care should be taken in the definition to avoid creating lists that may be interpreted as excluding potentially relevant "indoor" areas. It is recommended that "indoor" (or "enclosed") areas be defined to include any space covered by a roof or enclosed by one or more walls or sides, regardless of the type of material used for the roof, wall or sides, and regardless of whether the structure is permanent or temporary.

"Workplace"
A "workplace" should be defined broadly as "any place used by people during their employment or work". This should include not only work done for compensation, but also voluntary work, if it is of the type for which compensation is normally paid. In addition, "workplaces" include not only those places at which work is performed, but also all attached or associated

---

[1] It is possible that constituent elements of tobacco smoke may exist in air in amounts too small to be measured. Attention should be given to the possibility that the tobacco industry or the hospitality sector may attempt to exploit the limitations of this definition.

places commonly used by the workers in the course of their employment, including, for example, corridors, lifts, stairwells, lobbies, joint facilities, cafeterias, toilets, lounges, lunchrooms and also outbuildings such as sheds and huts. Vehicles used in the course of work are workplaces and should be specifically identified as such.

Careful consideration should be given to workplaces that are also individuals' homes or dwelling places, for example, prisons, mental health institutions or nursing homes. These places also constitute workplaces for others, who should be protected from exposure to tobacco smoke.

"Public transport"

Public transport should be defined to include any vehicle used for the carriage of members of the public, usually for reward or commercial gain. This would include taxis.

THE SCOPE OF EFFECTIVE LEGISLATION

Article 8 requires the adoption of effective measures to protect people from exposure to tobacco smoke in (1) indoor workplaces, (2) indoor public places, (3) public transport, and (4) "as appropriate" in "other public places".

This creates an *obligation to provide universal protection* by ensuring that all indoor public places, all indoor workplaces, all public transport and possibly other (outdoor or quasi-outdoor) public places are free from exposure to second-hand tobacco smoke. No exemptions are justified on the basis of health or law arguments. If exemptions must be considered on the basis of other arguments, these should be minimal. In addition, if a Party is unable to achieve universal coverage immediately, Article 8 creates a continuing obligation to move as quickly as possible to remove any exemptions and make the protection universal. Each Party should strive to provide universal protection within five years of the WHO FCTC's entry into force for that Party.

No safe levels of exposure to second-hand smoke exist, and, as previously acknowledged by the Conference of the Parties in decision FCTC/COP1(15), engineering approaches, such as ventilation, air exchange and the use of designated smoking areas, do not protect against exposure to tobacco smoke.

Protection should be provided in all indoor or enclosed workplaces, including motor vehicles used as places of work (for example, taxis, ambulances or delivery vehicles).

The language of the treaty requires protective measures not only in all "indoor" public places, but also in those "other" (that is, outdoor or quasi-outdoor) public places where "appropriate". In identifying those outdoor and quasi-outdoor public places where legislation is appropriate, Parties should consider the evidence as to the possible health hazards in various settings and should act to adopt the most effective protection against exposure wherever the evidence shows that a hazard exists.

INFORM, CONSULT AND INVOLVE THE PUBLIC TO ENSURE SUPPORT AND SMOOTH IMPLEMENTATION

Raising awareness among the public and opinion leaders about the risks of second-hand tobacco smoke exposure through ongoing information campaigns is an important role for government agencies, in partnership with civil society, to ensure that the public understands and supports legislative action. Key stakeholders include businesses, restaurant and hospitality associations, employer groups, trade unions, the media, health professionals, organizations representing children and young people, institutions of learning or faith, the research community and the general public. Awareness-raising efforts should include consultation with affected businesses and other organizations and institutions in the course of developing the legislation.

Key messages should focus on the harm caused by second-hand tobacco smoke exposure, the fact that elimination of smoke indoors is the only science-based solution to ensure complete protection from exposure, the right of all workers to be equally protected by law and the fact that there is no trade-off between health and economics, because experience in an increasing number of jurisdictions shows that smoke free environments benefit both. Public education campaigns should also target settings for which legislation may not be feasible or appropriate, such as private homes.

Broad consultation with stakeholders is also essential to educate and mobilize the community and to facilitate support for legislation after its enactment. Once legislation is adopted, there should be an education campaign leading up to implementation of the law, the provision of information for business owners and building managers outlining the law and their responsibilities and the production of resources, such as signage. These measures will increase the likelihood of smooth implementation and high levels of voluntary compliance. Messages to empower non-smokers and to thank smokers for complying with the law will promote public involvement in enforcement and smooth implementation.

ENFORCEMENT

Duty of compliance

Effective legislation should impose legal responsibilities for compliance on both affected business establishments and individual smokers, and should provide penalties for violations, which should apply to businesses and, possibly, smokers. Enforcement should ordinarily focus on business establishments. The legislation should place the responsibility for compliance on the owner, manager or other person in charge of the premises, and should clearly identify the actions he or she is required to take. These duties should include:

(a) a duty to post clear signs at entrances and other appropriate locations indicating that smoking is not permitted. The format and content of these signs should be determined by health authorities or other agencies of the government and may identify a telephone number or other mechanisms for the public to report violations and the name of the person within the premises to whom complaints should be directed;

(b) a duty to remove any ashtrays from the premises;

(c) a duty to supervise the observance of rules;

(d) a duty to take reasonable specified steps to discourage individuals from smoking on the premises. These steps could include asking the person not to smoke, discontinuing service, asking the person to leave the premises and contacting a law enforcement agency or other authority.

Penalties

The legislation should specify fines or other monetary penalties for violations. While the size of these penalties will necessarily reflect the specific practices and customs of each country, several principles should guide the decision. Most importantly, penalties should be sufficiently large to deter violations or else they may be ignored by violators or treated as mere costs of doing business. Larger penalties are required to deter business violators than to deter violations by individual smokers, who usually have fewer resources. Penalties should increase for repeated violations and should be consistent with a country's treatment of other, equally serious offences.

In addition to monetary penalties, the legislation may also allow for administrative sanctions, such as the suspension of business licences, consistent with the country's practice and legal system. These "sanctions of last resort" are rarely used, but are very important for enforcing the law against any businesses that choose to defy the law repeatedly.

Criminal penalties for violations may be considered for inclusion, if appropriate within a country's legal and cultural context.

Enforcement infrastructure

Legislation should identify the authority or authorities responsible for enforcement, and should include a system both for monitoring compliance and for prosecuting violators.

Monitoring should include a process for inspection of businesses for compliance. It is seldom necessary to create a new inspection system for enforcement of smoke free legislation. Instead, compliance can ordinarily be monitored using one or more of the mechanisms already in place for inspecting business premises and workplaces. A variety of options usually exists for this purpose. In many countries, compliance inspections may be integrated into business licensing inspections, health and sanitation inspections, inspections for workplace health and safety, fire safety inspections or similar programmes. It may be valuable to use several such sources of information gathering simultaneously.

Where possible, the use of inspectors or enforcement agents at the local level is recommended; this is likely to increase the enforcement resources available and the level of compliance. This approach requires the establishment of a national coordinating mechanism to ensure a consistent approach nationwide.

Regardless of the mechanism used, monitoring should be based on an overall enforcement plan, and should include a process for effective training of inspectors. Effective monitoring may combine regular inspections with unscheduled, surprise inspections, as well as visits made in response to complaints. Such visits may well be educative in the early period after the law takes effect, as most breaches are likely to be inadvertent. The legislation should authorize inspectors to enter premises subject to the law and to collect samples and gather evidence, if these powers are not already established by existing law. Similarly, the legislation should prohibit businesses from obstructing the inspectors in their work.

The cost of effective monitoring is not excessive. It is not necessary to hire large numbers of inspectors, because inspections can be accomplished using existing programmes and personnel, and because experience shows that smoke free legislation quickly becomes self-enforcing (that is, predominantly enforced by the public). Only a few prosecutions may be necessary if the legislation is implemented carefully and active efforts are made to educate businesses and the public.

Although these programmes are not expensive, resources are needed to educate businesses, train inspectors, coordinate the inspection process and compensate personnel for inspections of businesses outside of normal working hours. A funding mechanism should be identified for this purpose. Effective monitoring programmes have used a variety of funding sources, including dedicated tax revenues, business licensing fees and dedicated revenues from fines paid by violators.

Enforcement strategies

Strategic approaches to enforcement can maximize compliance, simplify the implementation of legislation and reduce the level of enforcement resources needed.

In particular, enforcement activities in the period immediately following the law's entrance into force are critical to the law's success and to the success of future monitoring and enforcement. Many jurisdictions recommend an initial period of soft enforcement, during which violators are cautioned but not penalized. This approach should be combined with an active campaign to educate business owners about their responsibilities under the law, and businesses should understand that the initial grace period or phase-in period will be followed by more rigorous enforcement.

When active enforcement begins, many jurisdictions recommend the use of high-profile prosecutions to enhance deterrence. By identifying prominent violators who have actively defied the law or who are well known in the community, by taking firm and swift action and by seeking maximum public awareness of these activities, authorities are able to demonstrate their resolve and the seriousness of the law. This increases voluntary compliance and reduces the resources needed for future monitoring and enforcement.

While smoke free laws quickly become self-enforcing, it is nevertheless essential that authorities be prepared to respond swiftly and decisively to any isolated instances of outright defiance. Particularly when a law first comes into force, there may be an occasional violator who makes a public display of contempt for the law. Strong responses in these cases set an expectation of compliance that will ease future efforts, while indecisiveness can rapidly lead to widespread violations.

Mobilize and involve the community

The effectiveness of a monitoring-and-enforcement programme is enhanced by involving the community in the programme. Engaging the support of the community and encouraging members of the community to monitor compliance and report violations greatly extends the reach of enforcement agencies and reduces the resources needed to achieve compliance. In fact, in many jurisdictions, community complaints are the primary means of ensuring compliance. For this reason, smoke free legislation should specify that members of the public may initiate complaints and should authorize any person or nongovernmental organization to initiate action to compel compliance with measures regulating exposure to second-hand smoke. The enforcement programme should include a toll-free telephone complaint hotline or a similar system to encourage the public to report violations.

MONITORING AND EVALUATION OF MEASURES

Monitoring and evaluation of measures to reduce exposure to tobacco smoke are important for several reasons, for example:

(a) to increase political and public support for strengthening and extending legislative provisions;

(b) to document successes that will inform and assist the efforts of other countries;

(c) to identify and publicize the efforts made by the tobacco industry to undermine the implementation measures.

The extent and complexity of monitoring and evaluation will vary among jurisdictions, depending on available expertise and resources. However, it is important to evaluate the outcome of the measures implemented, in particular, on the key indicator of exposure to second-hand smoke in workplaces and public places. There may be cost-effective ways to achieve this, for example through the use of data or information collected through routine activities such as workplace inspections.

There are eight key process and outcome indicators that should be considered:[2]

Processes

(a) knowledge, attitudes and support for smoke free policies among the general population and possibly specific groups, for example, bar workers;

(b) enforcement of and compliance with smoke free policies;

Outcomes

(c) reduction in exposure of employees to second-hand tobacco smoke in workplaces and public places;

(d) reduction in content of second-hand tobacco smoke in the air in workplaces (particularly in restaurants) and public places;

---

[2] The publication WHO policy recommendations: protection from exposure to second-hand tobacco smoke (Geneva, World Health Organization, 2007) provides references and links to monitoring studies conducted elsewhere on all of these indicators.

(e) reduction in mortality and morbidity from exposure to second-hand tobacco smoke;

(f) reduction in exposure to second-hand tobacco smoke in private homes;

(g) changes in smoking prevalence and smoking-related behaviours;

(h) economic impacts.

LINKS TO SAMPLE LEGISLATION AND RESOURCE DOCUMENTS

References to the national and sub-national legislations currently in force that most closely conform to these best practice guidelines are provided below:

(a) United Kingdom of Great Britain and Northern Ireland, Health Act 2006, http://www.opsi.gov.uk/acts/acts2006/20060028.htm

(b) New Zealand, Smoke-free Environments Amendment Act 2003, http://www.legislation.govt.nz/browse_vw.asp?content-set=pal_statutes

(c) Norway, Act No. 14 of 9 March 1973 relating to Prevention of the Harmful Effects of Tobacco,
http://odin.dep.no/hod/engelsk/regelverk/p20042245/042041-990030/dok-bn.html
   (It should be noted, however, that the option of smoking sections is not recommended under these guidelines.)

(d) Scotland, Smoking, Health and Social Care (Scotland) Act 2005, http://www.opsi.gov.uk/legislation/scotland/acts2005/20050013.htm
Regulations: http://www.opsi.gov.uk/si/si2006/20061115.htm

(e) Uruguay, Decreto 40/006, http://www.globalsmokefreepartnership.org/files/132.doc

(f) Ireland, Public Health (Tobacco) (Amendment) Act 2004, http://193.178.1.79/2004/en/act/pub/0006/index.html

(g) Bermuda, Tobacco Products (Public Health) Amendment Act 2005, http://www.globalsmokefreepartnership.org/files/139.DOC

Resource documents

1. WHO policy recommendations: protection from exposure to second-hand tobacco smoke. Geneva, World Health Organization, 2007.
http://www.who.int/tobacco/resources/publications/wntd/2007/who_ protection_exposure_ final_25June2007.pdf

2. Tobacco smoke and involuntary smoking. IARC Monographs on the Evolution of Carcinogenic Risks to Humans, Vol. 83, Lyon, France, World Health Organization and International Agency for Research on Cancer, 2004.
http://monographs.iarc.fr/ENG/Monographs/vol83/volume83.pdf

3. The health consequences of involuntary exposure to tobacco smoke: a report of the Surgeon General. Washington, DC, United States Department of Health and Human Services, 2006.
http://www.surgeongeneral.gov/library/secondhandsmoke/

4. Proposed identification of environmental tobacco smoke as a toxic air contaminant. San Francisco, United States of America, California Environmental Protection Agency: Air Resources Board, 2005.
http://repositories.cdlib.org/tc/surveys/CALEPA2005/

5. Joint briefing paper: Proposed guidelines for the implementation of Article 8 of the WHO Framework Convention on Tobacco Control. Framework Convention Alliance and the Global Smokefree Partnership, 2007.
http://www.fctc.org/x/documents/Article8_COP2_Briefing_English.pdf

6. Global Smokefree Partnership web site. A resource on smoke free success stories and challenges, this link includes perspectives on smoke free policies, links to evaluation reports, legislation and public information campaigns, as well as implementation guidelines.
www.globalsmokefreepartnership.org

7. After the smoke has cleared: evaluation of the impact of a new smoke free law. Wellington, New Zealand Ministry of Health, 2006.
http://www.moh.govt.nz/moh.nsf/by+unid/A9D3734516F6757ECC25723D0 0752D50?Open

Guidelines for implementation
Articles 9 and 10

Partial guidelines for implementation of Articles 9 and 10 of the WHO Framework Convention on Tobacco Control[1]

REGULATION OF THE CONTENTS OF TOBACCO PRODUCTS AND OF TOBACCO PRODUCT DISCLOSURES

1. PURPOSE, OBJECTIVES AND USE OF TERMS

1.1 Purpose

The purpose of the guidelines is to assist Parties in meeting their obligations under Articles 9 and 10 of the WHO Framework Convention on Tobacco Control (WHO FCTC). The guidelines, drawing on the best available scientific evidence and the experience of Parties, propose measures that may assist Parties in strengthening their tobacco-control policies through regulation of the contents and emissions of tobacco products and through regulation of tobacco product disclosures. Parties are also encouraged to implement measures beyond those recommended by these guidelines.[2]

Whereas Article 9 deals with the testing and measuring of the contents and emissions of tobacco products, and their regulation, Article 10 deals with the disclosure of information on such contents and emissions to governmental authorities and the public. Owing to the close relationship between these two articles, guidance for their implementation has been consolidated into one set of guidelines.

1.2 Objectives

1.2.1 Regulation of the contents and emissions of tobacco products

One objective of the guidelines is to support Parties in developing effective tobacco product regulation. Tobacco product regulation has the potential to contribute to reducing tobacco-attributable disease and premature death by reducing the attractiveness of tobacco products, reducing their addictiveness (or dependence liability) or reducing their overall toxicity.

1.2.1.1 Attractiveness

Tobacco products are commonly made to be attractive in order to encourage their use. From the perspective of public health, there is no justification for permitting the use of ingredients, such as flavouring agents, which help make tobacco products attractive. Other measures to reduce the attractiveness of

---

[1] As adopted by the COP at its fourth session in 2010, with amendments adopted at its fifth session in 2012.
[2] Parties are directed to the WHO FCTC web site (http://www.who.int/fctc/) where further sources of information on topics covered by these guidelines are maintained.

tobacco products have been included in the guidelines on the implementation of Articles 11 and 13 of the WHO FCTC.

The WHO FCTC, in its preamble, recognizes that tobacco products are harmful and create and maintain dependence. Any reduction of their attractiveness resulting from removing or reducing certain ingredients in no way suggests that those tobacco products are less dangerous for human health.

1.2.1.2 Addictiveness (dependence liability)

(This section has been left blank intentionally to indicate that guidance will be proposed at a later stage.[3])

1.2.1.3 Toxicity

(This section has been left blank intentionally to indicate that guidance will be proposed at a later stage.)

1.2.2 Disclosure to governmental authorities

Pursuant to Article 10, the primary objective of requiring disclosure to governmental authorities is to obtain from manufacturers and importers relevant information on the contents and emissions of tobacco products, as well as on their toxicity and addictiveness. This information is required for the development and implementation of relevant policies, activities and regulations, such as further analysis of tobacco product contents and emissions, monitoring of market trends, and assessment of tobacco industry claims.

1.2.3 Disclosure to the public

Pursuant to Article 10, the primary objective of public disclosure of information about the toxic constituents and emissions of tobacco products is to inform the public of the health consequences, addictive nature and mortal threat posed by tobacco consumption and exposure to tobacco smoke. This information may also assist the public in contributing to the development and implementation of relevant policies, activities and regulations.

1.3 Use of terms

"Attractiveness" refers to factors such as taste, smell and other sensory attributes, ease of use, flexibility of the dosing system, cost, reputation or image, assumed risks and benefits, and other characteristics of a product designed to stimulate use.[4]

---

[3] The guidelines are partial and will be completed in phases as new country experience, and scientific, medical and other evidence become available. Further progress will also depend on the validation of the analytical chemical methods for testing and measuring cigarette contents and emissions and other work pursuant to the decision by the Conference of Parties at its third session (decision FCTC/COP3(9)).

[4] WHO. The scientific basis of tobacco product regulation: Report of a WHO Study Group. WHO Technical Report Series 945. Geneva, World Health Organization, 2007.

"Contents" means "constituents" with respect to processed tobacco, and "ingredients" with respect to tobacco products. In addition:

- "Constituents":

(This section has been left blank intentionally to indicate that guidance will be proposed at a later stage.)

- "Ingredients" include tobacco, components (e.g. paper, filter), including materials used to manufacture those components, additives, processing aids, residual substances found in tobacco (following storage and processing), and substances that migrate from the packaging material into the product (contaminants are not part of the ingredients).

"Design feature" means a characteristic of the design of a tobacco product that has an immediate causal link with the testing and measuring of its contents and emissions. For example, ventilation holes around cigarette filters decrease machine-measured yields of nicotine by diluting mainstream smoke.

"Emissions" are substances that are released when the tobacco product is used as intended. For example, in the case of cigarettes and other combusted products, emissions are the substances found in the smoke. In the case of smokeless tobacco products for oral use, emissions are the substances released during the process of chewing or sucking, and in the case of nasal use, refer to substances released by particles during the process of snuffing.

"Expanded tobacco" is tobacco that has been expanded in volume by quick volatilization of a medium such as dry ice.

"Reconstituted tobacco" is a paper-like sheet material comprised mainly of tobacco.

"Tobacco industry" means, as defined in Article 1 of the WHO FCTC, "tobacco manufacturers, wholesale distributors and importers of tobacco products".

"Tobacco products", as defined in Article 1 of the WHO FCTC, are "products entirely or partly made of the leaf tobacco as raw material which are manufactured to be used for smoking, sucking, chewing, or snuffing".

2. PRACTICAL CONSIDERATIONS

2.1   Approval and implementation of measures pursuant to Article 9

As stated in Article 9 of the WHO FCTC, each Party shall, where approved by competent national authorities, adopt and implement effective legislative, executive and administrative or other measures, for the testing and measuring of the contents and emissions of tobacco products and for the regulation of these contents and emissions.

Parties should consider giving the authority responsible for tobacco control matters the responsibility for, or at a minimum the power to provide input into, the approval, adoption and implementation of the above-mentioned measures.

2.2 Approval and implementation of measures pursuant to Article 10

As stated in Article 10 of the WHO FCTC, each Party shall, in accordance with its national law, adopt and implement effective legislative, executive, administrative or other measures for the disclosure by manufacturers and importers of tobacco products to governmental authorities of information about the contents and emissions of tobacco products, as well as for the public disclosure of information about the toxic constituents of tobacco products and their emissions.

Parties should consider giving the authority responsible for tobacco control matters the responsibility for, or at a minimum the power to provide input into, the adoption and implementation of the above-mentioned measures.

2.3 Financing

Implementing effective tobacco product regulations and operating a programme for their administration require the allocation of significant resources by Parties. In order to alleviate governmental budgetary pressure, Parties could consider placing these costs on the tobacco industry and retailers. There are various means of financing tobacco product regulation measures.

The list below sets out some options that Parties could consider using:
- designated tobacco taxes;
- tobacco manufacturing and/or importing licensing fees;
- tobacco product registration fees;
- licensing of tobacco distributors and/or retailers;
- non-compliance fees levied on the tobacco industry and retailers; and
- annual tobacco surveillance fees (tobacco industry and retailers).

See Appendix 1 for descriptive examples of means of financing tobacco product regulation measures.

2.4 Laboratories used for purpose of disclosure

Laboratories used by manufacturers and importers of tobacco products for the purposes of disclosure to governmental authorities should be accredited in accordance with International Organization for Standardization (ISO) Standard 17025 (General requirements for the competence of testing and calibration laboratories), by a recognized accreditation body. The accreditation methods used should include, at a minimum, the methods set out in these guidelines.

2.5 Laboratories used for compliance purposes

Laboratories used by Parties for compliance purposes should be either governmental laboratories or independent laboratories that are not owned or controlled, directly or indirectly, by the tobacco industry. In addition, such laboratories should be accredited as set out in the previous paragraph. Parties may consider making use of governmental or independent laboratories located in other countries.

2.6 Confidentiality in relation to disclosure to governmental authorities

Parties should not accept claims from the tobacco industry concerning the confidentiality of information that would prevent governmental authorities from receiving information about the contents and emissions of tobacco products. Governmental authorities should apply appropriate rules in accordance with their national laws when collecting information claimed to be confidential by tobacco manufacturers and importers in order to prevent unauthorized use and/or dissemination of this information.[5]

2.7 Confidentiality in relation to disclosure to the public

Parties should disclose information about the toxic constituents and emissions of tobacco products to the public in a meaningful way. Parties may determine in accordance with their national laws the information about the toxic constituents and emissions of tobacco products that should not be disclosed to the public.

2.8 Civil society

Civil society has an important role to play in raising public awareness and building support for the regulation of the contents and emissions of tobacco products, and for the disclosure of information on these contents and emissions. Civil society should be involved as an active partner.

3. MEASURES

3.1 Content

3.1.1 Ingredients (Disclosure)

This section outlines measures that Parties could introduce to require the disclosure by manufacturers and importers of tobacco products of information about ingredients.

---

[5] Guidance regarding public disclosure of this information is left to future guidelines.

3.1.1.1 Background

By requiring manufacturers and importers to disclose information about ingredients to governmental authorities, valuable insight will be gained on the composition of tobacco products, which in turn will assist authorities in developing effective, product-appropriate measures.

3.1.1.2 Recommendations

(i) Parties should require that manufacturers and importers of tobacco products disclose to governmental authorities information on the ingredients used in the manufacture of their tobacco products at specified intervals, by product type and for each brand within a brand family. Contrary to disclosing ingredients as part of a combined list, disclosing on a brand-by-brand basis and in a standardized format will provide opportunities to governmental authorities to analyse trends in product composition and keep track of subtle changes in the market.

(ii) Parties should ensure that manufacturers and importers disclose to governmental authorities the ingredients used in the manufacture of each of their tobacco products and the quantities thereof per unit of each tobacco product, including those ingredients present in the product's components (e.g. filter, papers, glue), for each brand within a brand family. Parties should not accept disclosure only of maximum quantities by category of ingredient, or only of the total quantity. To do so would seriously limit the kind of analysis that could be performed.

(iii) Parties should require that manufacturers and importers disclose further information on the characteristics of the tobacco leaves they used, for example:

    (i) type(s) of tobacco leaves (e.g. Virginia, Burley, Oriental), and percentage of each type used in the tobacco product;

    (ii) percentage of reconstituted tobacco used;

    (iii) percentage of expanded tobacco used;

(iv) Parties should require that manufacturers and importers notify governmental authorities of any changes to tobacco product ingredients when the change is made;

(v) Parties should require that manufacturers and importers provide governmental authorities with a statement setting out the purpose[6]

---

[6] Examples include substances that are used as adhesives, binders, combustion modifiers, addictiveness enhancers, flavours, humectants, plasticizers, casings, smoke enhancers and colourings.

of the inclusion of an ingredient in the tobacco product and other relevant information;

(vi) Parties should require that manufacturers disclose the name, address and other contact information of each ingredient's supplier to facilitate direct disclosure to the Party by the supplier, where appropriate, and for compliance monitoring purposes.

3.1.2 Ingredients (Regulation)

This section outlines measures that Parties could introduce to regulate ingredients.

Parties should introduce the measures outlined in this section, in accordance with their national laws, taking into account their national circumstances and priorities.

Parties should consider scientific evidence, other evidence and experience of others countries when determining new measures on ingredients of tobacco products and they should aim to implement the most effective measures that they can achieve.

3.1.2.1 Background

Regulating ingredients aimed at reducing tobacco product attractiveness can contribute to reducing the prevalence of tobacco use and dependence among new and continuing users. The preamble to the WHO FCTC states that Parties recognize "that cigarettes and some other products containing tobacco are highly engineered so as to create and maintain dependence".

Attractiveness and its impact on dependence should be taken into account when considering regulatory measures. The guidelines on implementation of Article 13 of the WHO FCTC, on tobacco product advertising, promotion and sponsorship, recommend that restrictions apply to as many as possible of the features that make tobacco products more attractive to consumers. Such features include coloured cigarette papers and attractive smells. Similarly, this section presents measures that will help limit inducements to use tobacco.

3.1.2.2 Tobacco products

(i) Ingredients used to increase palatability

The harsh and irritating character of tobacco smoke provides a significant barrier to experimentation and initial use. Tobacco industry documents have shown that significant effort has been put into mitigating these unfavourable characteristics. Harshness can be reduced in a variety of ways including: adding various ingredients, eliminating substances with known irritant properties, balancing irritation alongside other significant sensory effects, or altering the chemical properties of tobacco product emissions by adding or removing specific substances.

Some tobacco products contain added sugars and sweeteners. High sugar content improves the palatability of tobacco products to tobacco users. Examples of sugars and sweeteners used in these products include glucose, molasses, honey and sorbitol.

Masking tobacco smoke harshness with flavours contributes to promoting and sustaining tobacco use. Examples of flavouring substances include benzaldehyde, maltol, menthol and vanillin.

Spices and herbs can also be used to improve the palatability of tobacco products. Examples include cinnamon, ginger and mint.

Recommendation:

Parties should regulate, by prohibiting or restricting, ingredients that may be used to increase palatability in tobacco products.

Ingredients indispensable for the manufacturing of tobacco products and not linked to attractiveness should be subject to regulation according to national law.

(ii) Ingredients that have colouring properties

Colouring agents are added to various components of tobacco products to make the resulting product more appealing. Attractively-coloured cigarettes (e.g. pink, black, denim blue) have been marketed in some countries. Examples of colouring agents include inks (e.g. imitation cork pattern on tipping paper) and pigments (e.g. titanium dioxide in filter material).

Recommendation:

Parties should prohibit or restrict ingredients that have colouring properties in tobacco products. However, Parties should consider allowing the use of colouring agents for tax-related markings or for health warnings and messages.

(iii) Ingredients used to create the impression that products have health benefits

Various ingredients have been used in tobacco products to help create the impression that such products have health benefits, or to create the impression that they present reduced health hazards. Examples include vitamins, such as vitamin C and vitamin E, fruit and vegetables (and products resulting from their processing such as fruit juices), amino acids, such as cysteine and tryptophan, and essential fatty acids such as omega-3 and omega-6.

Recommendation:

Parties should prohibit ingredients in tobacco products that may create the impression that they have a health benefit.

(iv) Ingredients associated with energy and vitality

Energy drinks, popular with young people in some parts of the world, are perceived to increase mental alertness and physical performance. Examples of stimulant compounds contained in such drinks include caffeine, guarana, taurine and glucuronolactone. Tobacco industry documents and patent applications show that some of these (caffeine and taurine) have also been considered for use in tobacco products.

Recommendation:

Parties should prohibit ingredients associated with energy and vitality, such as stimulant compounds, in tobacco products.

3.1.3 Constituents (Disclosure)

(This section has been left blank intentionally to indicate that guidance will be proposed at a later stage.)

3.1.4 Constituents (Regulation)

(This section has been left blank intentionally to indicate that guidance will be proposed at a later stage.)

3.2 Emissions

(This section has been left blank intentionally to indicate that guidance will be proposed at a later stage.)

3.3 Product characteristics

3.3.1 Disclosure

This section outlines measures that Parties could introduce to require the disclosure by manufacturers and importers of tobacco products of information about product characteristics, such as design features.

3.3.1.1 Background

Collecting data on product characteristics, such as design features, will help Parties improve their understanding of the impact these characteristics have on smoke emission levels, properly interpret measurements obtained and, more importantly, keep abreast of any changes to cigarette design features.

3.3.1.2 Recommendations

(i) Parties should require that manufacturers and importers of tobacco products disclose information on design features to governmental authorities at specified intervals, and as appropriate, including the results of tests conducted by the tobacco industry.

(ii) In order to establish and maintain the consistency of the data reported to them by the tobacco industry, Parties should specify the recommended methods, where applicable, for the reporting of design features as set out in Appendix 2.

(iii) Parties should ensure that every manufacturer and importer provides to governmental authorities a copy of the laboratory report where a laboratory test was performed for the measurement of a particular design feature, as well as the proof of accreditation of the laboratory that performed the analysis.

(iv) Should there be any change to the design features of a particular brand of tobacco product, Parties should require that manufacturers notify governmental authorities of the change and provide the updated information when the change is made.

3.3.2 Regulation

3.3.2.1 Cigarettes – Regulation in relation to fire-risk (reduced ignition propensity)

(i) Background

Lit cigarettes that are laid down and left unattended smoulder and can ignite upholstery, other furniture, bedding and other textiles, or other material. This has been observed most often in cases of smoking in bed or smoking while under the influence of alcohol, illicit drugs or medication. Every year a considerable number of people around the world are injured or die (e.g. from burns or smoke gas poisonings) as a result of fires caused by cigarettes.

In order to prevent a significant number of such injuries and deaths, cigarettes can be designed in a way that the cigarette self extinguishes when not puffed or left unattended and thereby has a reduced risk of starting fires. These cigarettes are known as reduced ignition propensity cigarettes (RIP cigarettes).

Reductions in the number of cigarette fires and related victims have been observed in some jurisdictions that have mandated the replacement of conventional cigarettes with RIP cigarettes. Although RIP cigarettes do not self-extinguish in every case, they are expected to reduce the risk of a fire being ignited, and thus the risk of injuries and deaths. It is important to note that mandating an RIP standard is aimed at reducing the number of fires caused by lit cigarettes; it will not eliminate them.

There have been claims that RIP cigarettes may have a different toxicity than conventional cigarettes. Research suggests that RIP cigarettes are just as toxic as conventional cigarettes and equally dangerous to human health.

(ii) Regulating the ignition propensity of cigarettes

In regulating the ignition propensity of cigarettes, governmental authorities usually take a performance-based approach by adopting provisions that prescribe the test method to be used, and then provisions that set the pass/fail criteria (performance standard) applicable to the results obtained after conduct of the test (see Appendix 4).

In a number of cases, governmental authorities have also laid down requirements related to a specific technique for achieving RIP, namely banded paper technology, and requirements related to certification (see Appendix 5).

(iii) Recommendations

(i) Parties should require that cigarettes comply with an RIP standard, taking into account their national circumstances and priorities.

(ii) When implementing recommendation (i) of this paragraph, Parties should consider setting a performance standard that corresponds at a minimum to the current international practice, regarding the percentage of cigarettes that may not burn their full length when tested according to the method described in Appendix 4.

(iii) Parties should not allow any claims to be made suggesting that RIP cigarettes would be unable to ignite fires.

3.4 Disclosure to governmental authorities – other information

3.4.1 Background

In order to put effective product regulation in place, including regulation of ingredients, it is essential that governmental authorities have accurate market information. Governmental authorities need to know the importance of a particular tobacco product compared to others to help determine regulatory needs and priorities. Furthermore, consistent with Article 20.2 of the WHO FCTC, information on tobacco companies and on their sales will help assess the magnitude and patterns of tobacco consumption.

3.4.2 Recommendations

Parties should require that manufacturers and importers of tobacco products disclose general company information, including the name, street address and contact information of the principal place of business and of each manufacturing and importing facility. This information may prove useful for compliance monitoring purposes.

Parties should consider requiring that tobacco manufacturers and importers disclose, at specified intervals, for each brand within a brand family, sales volume information in units (e.g. number of cigarettes or cigars, or weight of roll-your-own tobacco). These disclosures should be on a national basis, and where appropriate on a sub-national basis as well.

3.5 Disclosure to the public

3.5.1 Background

Many people are not fully aware of, misunderstand or underestimate the risks for morbidity and premature mortality attributable to tobacco use and exposure to tobacco smoke. Complementing other measures relating to the reduction of demand for tobacco, Article 10 of the WHO FCTC requires that each Party shall adopt and implement effective measures for public disclosure of information about the toxic constituents of tobacco products and the emissions that they may produce. As stated in Article 4.1 of the WHO FCTC, Parties shall be guided by the principle that every person should be informed of the health consequences, addictive nature and mortal threat posed by tobacco consumption and exposure to tobacco smoke.

3.5.2 Scope and means of public disclosure

3.5.2.1 *Public access to information disclosed to governmental authorities*

Detailed information about the toxic constituents and emissions of tobacco products is difficult to comprehend, and public disclosure of such information might not directly promote or protect public health. However, such information may assist other members of civil society, particularly academic institutions and nongovernmental organizations, in contributing to tobacco control policy.

In addition, other information disclosed to governmental authorities in accordance with these guidelines, such as information on ingredients, product characteristics and the market, may also contribute to raising public awareness and advancing tobacco control policy.

Recommendation:

Parties should consider, in accordance with their national laws, making information about the toxic constituents and emissions of tobacco products and other information disclosed to governmental authorities in accordance with these guidelines publicly accessible (e.g. via the Internet, or by request to a governmental authority) in a meaningful way.

3.5.2.2 *Public disclosure of constituents and emissions in the context of Articles 11 and 12 of the WHO FCTC*

Information on how public disclosure is linked to Articles 11 and 12 of the WHO FCTC can be found in section 7, "LINKS TO OTHER ARTICLES OF THE WHO FCTC".

4. COMPLIANCE AND ENFORCEMENT

4.1 Comprehensive approach

Effective legislative, executive, administrative or other measures should impose legal responsibilities for compliance on manufacturers and importers of tobacco products and should provide penalties for violations. Legislative, executive, administrative or other measures should identify the authority or authorities responsible for enforcement, and should include a system both for monitoring compliance and for prosecuting violators.

4.2 Infrastructure and budget

Parties should consider ensuring that the infrastructure necessary for compliance monitoring and enforcement activities exists. Parties should also consider providing a budget for such activities.

4.3 Strategies

To enhance compliance, Parties should inform stakeholders of the requirements of the law before it comes into force.

Parties should consider using inspectors or enforcement agents to conduct regular visits to manufacturing and importing facilities, as well as at points of sale, to ensure compliance. It may not be necessary to create a new inspection system if mechanisms are already in place that could be extended to inspect business premises as required.

4.4 Deadlines

4.4.1 Prohibited or restricted ingredients

Parties should specify a deadline following which tobacco industry and retailers must only supply tobacco products that comply with requirements.

4.4.2 Reduced ignition propensity

Parties should specify a deadline following which the tobacco industry and retailers must only supply cigarettes that comply with the required RIP standard.

4.5 Inspections – prohibited or restricted ingredients

Parties should consider conducting visits to manufacturing facilities to verify whether any prohibited or restricted ingredient is being used. Inspection should include direct access to the raw supplies storage area and to the finished products storage area, as well as direct observation of the manufacturing process. Inspections should not constitute an approval or certification of the tobacco products, nor recognition of their manufacturing procedures.

4.6 Sampling and testing

4.6.1 Prohibited or restricted ingredients

Parties should consider having samples of tobacco products collected from importers' facilities, from retail outlets and, where needed, from manufacturers' facilities. These samples should then be tested for the presence of prohibited or restricted ingredients in laboratories used for compliance purposes (see Appendix 3).

4.6.2 Reduced ignition propensity

Parties should consider having samples of cigarettes collected from manufacturers, importers or retailers. These samples should then be tested to ascertain whether they comply with the required RIP performance standard. Both sampling and testing should be carried out according to the method described in Appendix 4.

4.7 Audits following disclosure to governmental authorities

Parties should consider conducting audits at manufacturers' facilities to ensure that information received concerning tobacco products is complete and accurate. Audits should not constitute an approval or certification of the tobacco products, nor recognition of their manufacturing procedures.

4.8 Response to non-compliance

Parties should ensure that their enforcement authorities are prepared to respond quickly and decisively to instances of non-compliance. Strong, timely responses to early cases will make it clear that compliance is expected and will facilitate future enforcement. Parties should consider making the results of enforcement action public in order to send a strong message that non-compliance will be investigated and that appropriate action will be taken.

4.9 Sanctions

In order to deter non-compliance with the law, Parties should specify appropriate sanctions, such as criminal sanctions, monetary amounts, corrective actions, and the suspension, limitation or cancellation of business and import licences.

4.10 Seizure, forfeiture and destruction

Parties should ensure that they have authority to have non-compliant tobacco products seized, forfeited and destroyed, under supervision in accordance with national law.

4.11 Penalties

Parties should specify a range of fines or other penalties commensurate with the severity of the violation and whether it is a repeat violation.

5. INTERNATIONAL COOPERATION

International cooperation is essential if progress in tobacco product regulation and disclosure is to be made. Several articles of the WHO FCTC provide for the exchange of knowledge and experience to promote implementation. As stated in Article 22 of the WHO FCTC, such cooperation shall promote the transfer of technical, scientific and legal expertise and technology, as mutually agreed. It would result in the effective implementation of these guidelines and facilitate development of the best possible measures for regulating the contents of tobacco products.

6. MONITORING AND EVALUATION

(This section has been left blank intentionally to indicate that guidance will be proposed at a later stage.)

7. LINKS TO OTHER ARTICLES OF THE WHO FCTC

7.1 Packaging suggesting the presence of a prohibited ingredient

In the spirit of Articles 11 and 13 of the WHO FCTC, unless Parties have already adopted measures to ban any type of promotion on tobacco product packages (as outlined in the guidelines on Articles 11 and 13), Parties should consider imposing a ban on the sale of tobacco products whose packaging suggests the presence of an ingredient that has been prohibited or, where appropriate, restricted as per the above recommendations.

7.2 Information on relevant constituents and emissions on tobacco packaging

Tobacco product packaging and labelling are an effective means of public communication about constituents and emissions of tobacco products, as recognized in Article 11 of the WHO FCTC. Parties should refer to Article 11 and the guidelines for its implementation.

7.3 Information on relevant constituents and emissions in education, communication, training and other public awareness programmes

Parties should consider including messages about constituents and emissions of tobacco products in education, communication, training and other public awareness programmes. Such messages may reinforce efforts to inform the public of the health consequences, addictive nature and mortal threat posed by tobacco use and exposure to tobacco smoke in programmes established in accordance with Article 12 of the WHO FCTC and the guidelines for its implementation.

APPENDIX 1

Descriptive examples of means of financing tobacco product regulation measures

(a) Designated tobacco taxes

Designated tobacco taxes require a proportion of tobacco tax revenue to be allocated to a specified purpose or purposes, such as a tobacco-control programme or a health promotion fund. The proportion of tobacco tax revenue might be expressed as a percentage of revenue (e.g. 1%) or as a fixed monetary amount per unit (e.g. 25 cents per package of 20 cigarettes). Designated tobacco taxes are sometimes referred to as "earmarked tobacco taxes" or "hypothecated tobacco taxes".

(b) Tobacco manufacturing and/or importing licensing fees

A licensing fee on tobacco manufacturers and/or importers could be implemented in a number of ways. The fee could be a specified monetary amount per company, regardless of company size. (A separate fee might be required for each manufacturing and/or importing facility.) The fee could be a fixed monetary amount per unit sold (e.g. a certain amount per cigarette or package of cigarettes, or per gram for certain types of tobacco products). The fee could be based on a total amount for all companies, and determined on the basis of a company's market share (e.g. if the total amount to be paid by all companies was US$ 100 million and a company's market share was 20%, and the company's license fee would be US$ 20 million). The required fee might have to be paid at specified intervals, such as prior to the beginning of an annual period. Where a fee is based on a monetary amount per unit sold, the payment interval might be more frequent, e.g. monthly.

(c) Tobacco product registration fees

Tobacco product registration fees involve requiring the manufacturer and/or importer, or potentially a wholesale distributor, to register each tobacco product sold by the company and to pay an accompanying fee. The amount of the fee might be set at a level such that government costs (or average costs) associated with the product, such as testing, measuring and enforcement, are fully or partially recovered. The required fee might have to be paid at specified intervals, e.g. prior to the beginning of an annual period.

(d) Licensing of tobacco distributors and/or retailers

A licensing fee could be placed on distributors or retailers, or both. The fee could be a specified monetary amount per outlet, regardless of company size. (A separate fee might be required for each manufacturing and/or importing facility.) The fee could vary based on the size of the distributor and/or retailer, e.g. based on sales volume. The fee might be set at varying amounts depending on sales volume (either units or total monetary amount), e.g. a fee if sales are not higher than amount A, a higher fee if sales are between amount A and amount B, and a further increased fee if sales are higher than amount B. The required fee might have to be paid at specified intervals, e.g. prior to the beginning of an annual period.

(e) Non-compliance fees levied on the tobacco industry and retailers

Revenue could be collected from administrative monetary penalties. Administrative monetary penalties are a form of civil penalty in which an administrative body seeks monetary relief against an individual or corporate body as restitution for unlawful activity. Revenue could also be collected from fines imposed by a court.

(f) Annual tobacco surveillance fees (tobacco industry and retailers)

Annual tobacco surveillance fees involve assessing the amount to be paid by the tobacco industry and/or retailers for monitoring and enforcement. For tobacco manufacturers/importers/distributors, this could be a fixed amount per company, a fixed amount for each brand variation sold, a fixed amount per unit sold, or an amount based on market share. For tobacco retailers (or others), a separate licence and fee might be required for each retail outlet.

APPENDIX 2

Design features of cigarettes[7]

- Dimensions, diameter and weight
- Length of filter, shape of the cross-section of the filter
- Length of tipping paper
- Dimensions and shape of the cross-section of the tobacco rod
- Distance of ventilation holes from butt mark in millimetres
- Draw resistance of cigarette as determined in accordance with ISO 6565 (Tobacco and tobacco products – Draw resistance of cigarettes and pressure drop of filter rods – Standard conditions and measurement)
- Degree of filter ventilation as determined in accordance with ISO 9512 (Cigarettes –Determination of ventilation – Definitions and measurement principles)
- Degree of paper ventilation as determined in accordance with ISO 9512 (Cigarettes – Determination of ventilation – Definitions and measurement principles)
- Type of cigarette paper used and its air permeability or porosity determined in accordance with ISO 2965 (Materials used as cigarette papers, filter plug wrap and filter joining paper, including

---

[7] See ISO 9512 (Cigarettes — Determination of ventilation — Definitions and measurement principles) for an explanation of the terms used here.

materials having an oriented permeable zone – Determination of air permeability)
- Product firmness (nominally a measure of packing density)
- Pressure drop of the filter as determined in accordance with ISO 6565 (Tobacco and tobacco products – Draw resistance of cigarettes and pressure drop of filter rods – Standard conditions and measurement)
- Moisture content as determined in accordance with Association of Official Analytical Chemists Official Method 966.02 (Loss on drying (moisture) in tobacco)[8]
- Type of filter (for example, cellulose acetate) and other characteristics, where applicable (for example, charcoal content)

APPENDIX 3

Analytical methods for ingredients

(a) For the purposes of compliance monitoring and enforcement, there may be cases in which analytical methods would be required to confirm the presence of prohibited or restricted ingredients. Such methods typically consist of several distinct steps: sampling, sample preparation, separation, identification, quantification and data analysis.

(b) Analytical procedures should be carried out by properly trained personnel in a suitably equipped laboratory. Such procedures frequently involve the use of hazardous materials. To ensure the correct and safe execution of these procedures, it is essential that laboratory personnel follow standard safety procedures for the handling of hazardous materials.

(c) For ingredients that are also food additives, suitable analytical methods may be found in the *Combined compendium of food additive specifications (volume 4)*.[9] This document provides a reference for the analytical methods mentioned in the specifications for the identity of additives used in foods or in food production.

(d) For ingredients such as flavouring agents which have a low-boiling point (that is, which vaporize easily at low temperatures), a technique called "headspace-gas chromatography" may be used. A description of this method may be found in the *Combined compendium of food additive specifications (volume 4)*.

(e) Another laboratory technique for sampling ingredients with a low boiling point, which can be combined for separation, identification and quantification with gas chromatography/mass spectrometry, is called "solid-phase

---

[8] See Horwitz W, Latimer G, eds. *Official methods of analysis*, 18th ed., Revision 3. Gaithersburg, MD, AOAC International, 2010.
[9] Joint FAO/WHO Expert Committee on Food Additives. *Combined compendium of food additive specifications. Volume 4: analytical methods, test procedures and laboratory solutions used by and referenced in the food additive specifications.* Rome, Food and Agriculture Organization of the United Nations, 2006 (FAO JECFA Monograph No. 1) (http://www.fao.org/docrep/009/a0691e/A0691E00.htm, accessed 1 April 2010).

microextraction".[10] It is very similar to headspace analysis, but differs in that the headspace is concentrated.

APPENDIX 4

Performance standard for reduced ignition propensity (RIP) cigarettes and related standard test methods

The performance standard for RIP cigarettes has been expressed as the percentage of cigarettes that, when ignited and laid down on a pre-determined substrate, do not burn through their whole length.

As of 2012, international practice is to require a not-burn-through rate of no less than 75%.

As of 2012, available standard test methods for sampling and verifying the conformity of cigarettes with the required not-burn-through rate include: ISO 12863:2010 "Standard test method for assessing the ignition propensity of cigarettes"; EN ISO 12863:2010 "Standard test method for assessing the ignition propensity of cigarettes"; AS 4830-2007 "Determination of the extinction propensity of cigarettes"; NZS/AS 4830:2007 "Determination of the extinction propensity of cigarettes"; and ASTM E2187-09 "Standard Test Method for Measuring the Ignition Strength of Cigarettes".

APPENDIX 5

Reduced ignition propensity cigarettes – additional information

(a) Design of the cigarette paper

Where Parties have required banded paper technology, one of the practices with respect to both filter and non-filter cigarettes is for one band surrounding the tobacco column to be located not less than 15 mm from the lighting end of the cigarette, and for a second such band to be located not less than 10 mm from the filter end or, in the case of non-filter cigarettes, not less than 10 mm from the labelled end of the tobacco column.

(b) Certification approach

Where a self-certification approach has been adopted, the practice is to require the tobacco industry to file with the appropriate governmental authority a statement of conformity and/or declaration of truth, with the required RIP standard. An alternative approach would be to mandate third-party certification.

---

[10] Pawliszyn J et al. Solid-phase microextraction (SPME). *The chemical educator*, 1997, 2(4):1–7 (http://www.springerlink.com/content/h72xx3624q122085/fulltext.pdf, accessed 1 April 2010).

Guidelines for implementation
Article 11

Guidelines for implementation of Article 11 of the WHO Framework Convention on Tobacco Control

PACKAGING AND LABELLING OF TOBACCO PRODUCTS

PURPOSE, PRINCIPLES AND USE OF TERMS

Purpose

Consistent with other provisions of the WHO Framework Convention on Tobacco Control and the intentions of the Conference of the Parties to the Convention, these guidelines are intended to assist Parties in meeting their obligations under Article 11 of the Convention, and to propose measures that Parties can use to increase the effectiveness of their packaging and labelling measures. Article 11 stipulates that each Party shall adopt and implement effective packaging and labelling measures within a period of three years after entry into force of the Convention for that Party.

Principles

In order to achieve the objectives of the Convention and its protocols and to ensure successful implementation of its provisions, Article 4 of the Convention states that Parties shall be guided, inter alia, by the principle that every person should be informed of the health consequences, addictive nature and mortal threat posed by tobacco consumption and exposure to tobacco smoke.

Globally, many people are not fully aware of, misunderstand or underestimate the risks for morbidity and premature mortality due to tobacco use and exposure to tobacco smoke. Well-designed health warnings and messages on tobacco product packages have been shown to be a cost-effective means to increase public awareness of the health effects of tobacco use and to be effective in reducing tobacco consumption. Effective health warnings and messages and other tobacco product packaging and labelling measures are key components of a comprehensive, integrated approach to tobacco control.

Parties should consider the evidence and the experience of others when determining new packaging and labelling measures and aim to implement the most effective measures they can achieve.

As provided for in Articles 20 and 22 of the Convention, international collaboration and mutual support are fundamental principles for strengthening the capacity of Parties to implement fully and improve the effectiveness of Article 11 of the Convention.

Use of terms

For the purposes of these guidelines:

> "legal measures" means any legal instrument that contains or establishes obligations, requirements or prohibitions, according to the law of the relevant jurisdiction. Examples of such instruments include, but are not limited to acts, laws, regulations and administrative or executive orders;
>
> "insert" means any communication inside an individual package and/or carton purchased at retail by consumers, such as a miniature leaflet or brochure.
>
> "onsert" means any communication affixed to the outside of an individual package and/or carton purchased at retail by consumers, such as a miniature brochure beneath the outer cellophane wrapping or glued to the outside of the cigarette package.

DEVELOPING EFFECTIVE PACKAGING AND LABELLING REQUIREMENTS

Well-designed health warnings and messages are part of a range of effective measures to communicate health risks and to reduce tobacco use. Evidence demonstrates that the effectiveness of health warnings and messages increases with their prominence. In comparison with small, text-only health warnings, larger warnings with pictures are more likely to be noticed, better communicate health risks, provoke a greater emotional response and increase the motivation of tobacco users to quit and to decrease their tobacco consumption. Larger picture warnings are also more likely to retain their effectiveness over time and are particularly effective in communicating health effects to low-literacy populations, children and young people. Other elements that enhance effectiveness include locating health warnings and messages on principal display areas, and at the top of these principal display areas; the use of colour rather than just black and white; requiring that multiple health warnings and messages appear concurrently; and periodic revision of health warnings and messages.

Design elements

Location

Article 11.1(b)(iii) of the Convention specifies that each Party shall adopt and implement effective measures to ensure that health warnings and messages are large, clear, visible and legible. The location and layout of health warnings and messages on a package should ensure maximum visibility. Research indicates that health warnings and messages are more visible at the top rather than the bottom of the front and back of packages. Parties should require that health warnings and messages be positioned:

> on both the front and back (or on all main faces if there are more than two) of each unit packet and package, rather than just one side, to ensure that health warnings and messages are highly visible, recognizing that the frontal display area is the one most visible to the user for most package types;
>
> on principal display areas and, in particular, at the top of the principal display areas rather than at the bottom to increase visibility; and
>
> in such a way that normal opening of the package does not permanently damage or conceal the text or image of the health warning.

Parties should consider requiring, in addition to the health warnings and messages referred to in the previous paragraph, further health warnings and messages on all sides of a package, as well as on package inserts and onserts.

Parties should ensure that health warnings and messages are not obstructed by other required packaging and labelling markings or by commercial inserts and onserts. Parties should also ensure, when establishing the size and position of other markings, such as tax stamps and markings as per the requirements of Article 15 of the Convention, that such markings do not obstruct any part of the health warnings and messages.

Parties should consider introducing other innovative measures regarding location, including, but not limited to, requiring health warnings and messages to be printed on the filter overwrap portion of cigarettes and/or on other related materials such as packages of cigarette tubes, filters and papers as well as other instruments, such as those used for water pipe smoking.

Size

Article 11.1(b)(iv) of the Convention specifies that health warnings and messages on tobacco product packaging and labelling should be 50% or more, but no less than 30%, of the principal display areas. Given the evidence that the effectiveness of health warnings and messages increases with their size, Parties should consider using health warnings and messages that cover more than 50% of the principal display areas and aim to cover as much of the principal display areas as possible. The text of health warnings and messages should be in bold print in an easily legible font size and in a specified style and colour(s) that enhance overall visibility and legibility.

If a border is required, Parties should consider excluding the space dedicated to framing health warnings and messages from the size of the health warning or message itself when calculating the percentage of display area occupied by them, that is to say the space dedicated to the frame should be added to the total percentage of space occupied by the health warnings and messages and not included within it.

Use of pictorials

Article 11.1(b)(v) of the Convention specifies that health warnings and messages on tobacco product packaging and labelling may be in the form of or include pictures or pictograms. Evidence shows that health warnings and messages that contain both pictures and text are far more effective than those that are text-only. They also have the added benefit of potentially reaching people with low levels of literacy and those who cannot read the language(s) in which the text of the health warning or message is written. Parties should mandate culturally appropriate pictures or pictograms, in full colour, in their packaging and labelling requirements. Parties should consider the use of pictorial health warnings on both principal display areas (or on all main faces if there are more than two) of the tobacco products packaging.

Evidence shows that, when compared with text-only health warnings and messages, those with pictures:

- are more likely to be noticed;
- are rated more effective by tobacco users;
- are more likely to remain salient over time;
- better communicate the health risks of tobacco use;
- provoke more thought about the health risks of tobacco use and about cessation;
- increase motivation and intention to quit; and
- are associated with more attempts to quit.

Pictorial health warnings and messages may also disrupt the impact of brand imagery on packaging and decrease the overall attractiveness of the package.

When creating pictures for use on tobacco product packaging, Parties should obtain, where possible, ownership or full copyright of images, instead of allowing graphic designers or other sources to retain copyright. This provides maximum flexibility to use the images for other tobacco control interventions, including mass media campaigns and on the Internet. It may also enable Parties to grant licences to other jurisdictions to use the images.

Colour

The use of colour, as opposed to black and white, affects the overall noticeability of pictorial elements of health warnings and messages. Therefore, Parties should require full colour (four-colour printing), rather than black and white, for pictorial elements of health warnings and messages. Parties should select contrasting colours for the background of the text in order to enhance noticeability and maximize the legibility of text-based elements of health warnings and messages.

Rotation

Article 11.1(b)(ii) of the Convention specifies that health warnings and messages shall be rotating. Rotation can be implemented by having multiple health warnings and messages appearing concurrently or by setting a date after which the health warning and message content will change. Parties should consider using both types of rotation.

The novelty effect of new health warnings and messages is important, as evidence suggests that the impact of health warnings and messages that are repeated tends to decrease over time, whereas changes in health warnings and messages are associated with increased effectiveness. Rotation of health warnings and messages and changes in their layout and design are important to maintain saliency and enhance impact.

Parties should specify the number of health warnings and messages that are to appear concurrently. Parties should also require that health warnings and messages in a specified series be printed so that each appears on an equal number of retail packages, not just for each brand family but also for each brand within the brand family for each package size and type.

Parties should consider establishing two or more sets of health warnings and messages, specified from the outset, to alternate after a specified period, such as every 12–36 months. During transition periods, when an old set of health warnings and messages is being replaced by a new set, Parties should provide for a phase-in period for rotation between sets of health warnings and messages, during which time both sets may be used concurrently.

Message content

Using a range of health warnings and messages increases the likelihood of impact, as different health warnings and messages resonate with different people. Health warnings and messages should address different issues related to tobacco use, in addition to harmful health effects and the impact of exposure to tobacco smoke, such as:

- advice on cessation;
- the addictive nature of tobacco;
- adverse economic and social outcomes (for example, annual cost of purchasing tobacco products); and
- the impact of tobacco use on significant others (premature illness of one's father due to smoking, for example, or death of a loved one due to exposure to tobacco smoke).

Parties should also consider innovative content for other messages, such as adverse environmental outcomes and tobacco industry practices.

It is important to convey health warnings and messages in an effective manner; the tone should be authoritative and informative but non-judgemental. Health warnings and messages should also be presented in simple, clear and concise language that is culturally appropriate. Health warnings and messages can be presented in various formats, such as testimonials and positive and supportive information.

Evidence suggests that health warnings and messages are likely to be more effective if they elicit unfavourable emotional associations with tobacco use and when the information is personalized to make the health warnings and messages more believable and personally relevant. Health warnings and messages that generate negative emotions such as fear can be effective, particularly when combined with information designed to increase motivation and confidence in tobacco users in their ability to quit.

The provision of advice on cessation and specific sources for cessation help on tobacco packaging, such as a web site address or a toll-free telephone "quit line" number, can be important in helping tobacco users to change their behaviour. Parties should be aware that an increased demand for cessation-related services might require additional resources.

Language

Article 11.3 of the Convention specifies that each Party shall require that the warnings and other textual information specified in Article 11.1(b) and Article 11.2 appear on each unit packet and package of tobacco products, as well as on any outside packaging and labelling of such products, in the Party's principal language or languages.

In jurisdictions where there is more than one principal language, health warnings and messages can be displayed on each principal display area in more than one language, or, alternatively, a different language can be used for different principal display areas. Where appropriate, different languages or language combinations could also be used in different regions of a jurisdiction.

Source attribution

An attribution statement gives an identified source for the health warnings and messages on tobacco product packaging. There are, however, mixed views about whether they should form part of health warnings and messages. Some jurisdictions have provided a source attribution statement in order to increase the credibility of the health warnings and messages, while others have decided not to include a source attribution out of concern that it might detract from the impact of the warning. Where a source attribution statement is required, it is often located at the end of the health warning, in a smaller font size than the rest of the warning. Ultimately, Party-specific circumstances, such as beliefs and attitudes among target population subgroups, will determine whether the use of source attribution is likely to increase credibility or reduce impact.

If required, a source attribution statement should specify a credible expert source, such as the national health authority. The statement should be small enough not to detract from the overall noticeability and impact of the message, while being large enough to be legible.

Information on constituents and emissions

Article 11.2 of the Convention specifies that each unit packet and package of tobacco products, and any outside packaging and labelling of such products, shall, in addition to the warnings specified in Article 11.1(b), contain information on relevant constituents and emissions of tobacco products as defined by national authorities.

In implementing this obligation, Parties should require that relevant qualitative statements be displayed on each unit packet or package about the emissions of the tobacco product. Examples of such statements include "smoke from these cigarettes contains benzene, a known cancer-causing substance" and "smoking exposes you to more than 60 cancer-causing chemicals". Parties should also require that this information be shown on parts of the principal display areas or on an alternative display area (such as the side of packaging) not occupied by health warnings and messages.

Parties should not require quantitative or qualitative statements on tobacco product packaging and labelling about tobacco constituents and emissions that might imply that one brand is less harmful than another, such as the tar, nicotine and carbon monoxide figures or statements such as "these cigarettes contain reduced levels of nitrosamines".

The above three paragraphs should be read in conjunction with paragraphs below on "Preventing packaging and labelling that is misleading or deceptive".

PROCESS FOR DEVELOPING EFFECTIVE PACKAGING AND LABELLING REQUIREMENTS

Product category considerations

Article 11.1(b) of the Convention requires each Party to adopt and implement effective measures to ensure that each unit packet or package of tobacco products and any outside packaging and labelling of such products carry health warnings and messages. There should be no exemptions for small-volume companies or brands or for different types of tobacco products. Parties should consider requiring different health warnings and messages for different tobacco products such as cigarettes, cigars, smokeless tobacco, pipe tobacco, bidis and water pipe tobacco, in order to better focus on the specific health effects related to each product.

Different types of packaging

Parties should have a comprehensive understanding of the many different types of tobacco product packaging found within their jurisdiction, and should indicate how the proposed health warnings and messages will apply to each type and shape of packaging such as tins, boxes, pouches, flip-tops, slide and shell packages, cartons, transparent wrappers, clear packaging or packages containing one product unit.

Targeting population subgroups

Parties should consider designing warnings that target subgroups, such as youth, and adapting the number of health warnings and their rotation accordingly.

Pre-marketing testing

Depending on the available resources and time, Parties should consider pre-marketing testing to assess the effectiveness of the health warnings and messages on the intended target population. Pre-marketing testing can permit identification of unintended effects, such as inadvertently increasing the craving to smoke, and assessment of their cultural appropriateness. Consideration should be given to inviting civil society organizations not affiliated with the tobacco industry to contribute to this process. Ultimately, pre-marketing testing can be less costly than changes to legal measures at a later stage.

Parties should note that pre-marketing testing need not be long, complex or expensive. Valuable information can be obtained from simple focus groups of the target population, and Internet-based consultation is a quick and inexpensive alternative. Pre-marketing testing can be undertaken in parallel with the drafting of legal measures to avoid undue delay in implementation.

Public information and involvement

Parties should inform the public of proposals to introduce new health warnings and messages. Public support will assist Parties in introducing the new health warnings and messages. Parties should ensure, however, that public information and involvement do not unduly delay implementation of the Convention.

Supporting communication activity

The introduction of new health warnings and messages is more effective when it is coordinated with a broader, sustained public information and education campaign. Timely information should be provided to the media, as media coverage can increase the educational impact of new health warnings and messages.

DEVELOPING EFFECTIVE PACKAGING AND LABELLING RESTRICTIONS

Preventing packaging and labelling that is misleading or deceptive

Article 11.1(a) of the Convention specifies that Parties shall adopt and implement, in accordance with their national law, effective measures to ensure that tobacco product packaging and labelling do not promote a tobacco product by any means that are false, misleading, deceptive or likely to create an erroneous impression about the product's characteristics, health effects, hazards or emissions, including any term, descriptor, trademark or figurative or other sign that directly or indirectly creates the false impression that a particular tobacco product is less harmful than others. These may include terms such as "low tar", "light", "ultra-light" or "mild", this list being indicative but not exhaustive. In implementing the obligations pursuant to Article 11.1(a), Parties are not limited to prohibiting the terms specified but should also prohibit terms such as "extra", "ultra" and similar terms in any language that might mislead consumers.

Parties should prohibit the display of figures for emission yields (such as tar, nicotine and carbon monoxide) on packaging and labelling, including when used as part of a brand name or trademark. Tar, nicotine and other smoke emission yields derived from smoking-machine testing do not provide valid estimates of human exposure. In addition, there is no conclusive epidemiological or scientific evidence that cigarettes with lower machine-generated smoke yields are less harmful than cigarettes with higher smoke emission yields. The marketing of cigarettes with stated tar and nicotine yields has resulted in the mistaken belief that those cigarettes are less harmful.

Parties should prevent the display of expiry dates on tobacco packaging and labelling where this misleads or deceives consumers into concluding that tobacco products are safe to be consumed at any time.

Plain packaging

Parties should consider adopting measures to restrict or prohibit the use of logos, colours, brand images or promotional information on packaging other than brand names and product names displayed in a standard colour and font style (plain packaging). This may increase the noticeability and effectiveness of health warnings and messages, prevent the package from detracting attention from them, and address industry package design techniques that may suggest that some products are less harmful than others.

LEGAL MEASURES

Drafting

In drafting legal measures with respect to tobacco product packaging and labelling, Parties should consider issues such as who will be responsible for their administration, the available approaches for ensuring compliance and enforcement, and the level or levels of government involved.

Administration

Parties should identify the authority or authorities responsible for overseeing implementation of tobacco product packaging and labelling measures. Parties should consider ensuring that the relevant authority responsible for tobacco control matters is the same as that which administers the legal measures. In the event that the administration is made the responsibility of another area of government, the relevant health authority should provide input into label specifications.

Scope

Parties should ensure that the packaging and labelling provisions related to Article 11 of the Convention apply equally to all tobacco products sold within the jurisdiction, and that no distinction is made between products that are manufactured domestically or imported or intended for duty-free sale within a Party's jurisdiction. Parties should consider circumstances in which measures would apply to exported products.

Costs

Parties should ensure that the cost of placing health warnings and messages, as well as information on constituents and emissions, on tobacco product packaging is borne by the tobacco industry.

Liability

Consistent with Article 19 of the Convention, Parties should consider including provisions to make it clear that the requirement to carry health warnings and messages or to convey any other information about a tobacco product does not remove or diminish any obligation of the tobacco industry, including, but not limited to, obligations to warn consumers about the health hazards arising from tobacco use and exposure to tobacco smoke.

Specific provisions

Parties should ensure that clear, detailed specifications are provided for in their legal measures in order to limit the opportunity for tobacco manufacturers and importers to deviate in the implementation of health warnings and messages, as well as to prevent inconsistencies among tobacco products. In drafting such measures, Parties should review, inter alia, the following list:

> packaging and products (please refer to paragraph above on "Different types of packaging");
>
> language(s) to be used in mandated text of health warnings and messages and in information on constituents and emissions on packaging, including how languages should appear if there is more than one language;
>
> rotation practice and time frames, including the number of health warnings and messages to appear concurrently as well as specifications of transition periods and deadlines within which the new health warnings and messages must appear;
>
> distribution practices, in order to obtain equal display of health warnings and messages on retail packages, not just for each brand family but also for each brand within the brand family for each package size and type;
>
> how text, pictures and pictograms of health warnings and messages should actually appear on packaging (including specification of location, wording, size, colour, font, layout, print quality), including package inserts, onserts and interior messages;
>
> different health warnings and messages for different types of tobacco product, where appropriate;
>
> source attribution, if appropriate, including placement, text and font (similar detailed specifications as for the health warnings and messages themselves); and
>
> prohibition of promotion by means that are false, misleading, deceptive or likely to create an erroneous impression, in accordance with Article 11.1(a) of the Convention.

Source document

Parties should consider providing a "source document", which contains high-quality visual samples of how all health warnings and messages and other information are to appear on packaging. A source document is particularly useful in the event that the language used in the legal measures is not sufficiently clear.

Adhesive labels and covers

Parties should ensure that adhesive labels, stickers, cases, covers, sleeves, wrapping and tobacco manufacturers' promotional inserts and onserts do not obscure, obliterate or undermine health warnings and messages. For example, adhesive labels might be allowed only if they cannot be removed and are used only on metal or wood containers that hold products other than cigarettes.

Legal responsibility for compliance

Parties should specify that tobacco product manufacturers, importers, wholesalers and retail establishments that sell tobacco products bear legal responsibility for compliance with packaging and labelling measures.

Penalties

In order to deter non-compliance with the law, Parties should specify a range of fines or other penalties commensurate with the severity of the violation and whether it is a repeat violation.

Parties should consider introducing any other penalty consistent with a Party's legal system and culture that may include the creation and enforcement of offences and the suspension, limitation or cancellation of business and import licences.

Enforcement powers

Parties should consider granting enforcement authorities the power to order violators to recall non-compliant tobacco products, and to recover all expenses stemming from the recall, as well as the power to impose whatever sanctions are deemed appropriate, including seizure and destruction of non-compliant products. Further, Parties should consider making public the names of violators and the nature of their offence.

Supply deadline

In order to ensure the timely introduction of health warnings and messages, legal measures should specify a single deadline by which manufacturers, importers, wholesalers and retailers must only supply tobacco products that comply with the new requirements. The time allocated need only be enough to allow manufacturers and importers to organize the printing of new packages. It has been considered that a period of up to 12 months from the enactment of the legal measures should suffice in most circumstances.

Review

Parties should recognize that the drafting of legal measures for packaging and labelling of tobacco products is not a one-time exercise. Legal measures should be reviewed periodically and updated as new evidence emerges and as specific health warnings and messages wear out. When undertaking periodic reviews or updates, Parties should take into account their experience in using their packaging and labelling measures, the experiences of other jurisdictions, as well as industry practices in this area. Such reviews or updates can help identify weaknesses and loopholes and highlight areas in which the language used in the measures should be clarified.

ENFORCEMENT

Infrastructure and budget

Parties should consider ensuring that the infrastructure necessary for compliance and enforcement activities exists. Parties should also consider providing a budget for such activities.

Strategies

To enhance compliance, Parties should inform stakeholders of the requirements of the law before it comes into force. Different strategies might be required for different stakeholders, such as tobacco manufacturers, importers and retailers.

Parties should consider using inspectors or enforcement agents to conduct regular spot checks of tobacco products at manufacturing and importing facilities, as well as at points of sale, to ensure that packaging and labelling comply with the law. It may not be necessary to create a new inspection system if mechanisms are already in place that could be extended to inspect business premises as required. Where applicable, stakeholders should be informed that tobacco products will undergo regular spot checks at points of sale.

Response to non-compliance

Parties should ensure that their enforcement authorities are prepared to respond quickly and decisively to instances of non-compliance. Strong, timely responses to early cases will make it clear that compliance is expected and will facilitate future enforcement. Parties should consider making the results of enforcement action public in order to send a strong message that non-compliance will be investigated and action will be taken.

Complaints

Parties should consider encouraging the public to report violations in order to further promote compliance with the law. It might be helpful to establish an enforcement contact point for reporting alleged cases of non-compliance. Parties should ensure that complaints are investigated and dealt with in a timely and thorough manner.

MONITORING AND EVALUATING PACKAGING AND LABELLING MEASURES

Parties should consider monitoring and evaluating their packaging and labelling measures to assess their impact as well as to identify where improvements are needed. Monitoring and evaluation also contribute to the body of evidence that can assist the efforts of other Parties in implementing their packaging and labelling measures.

Monitoring of the tobacco industry's compliance should be initiated immediately after legal measures have come into force and should be conducted continuously thereafter.

Impact on populations

It is important to assess the impact of packaging and labelling measures on the target populations. Parties should consider measuring aspects such as noticeability, comprehension, credibility, informativeness, recall and personal relevance of health warnings and messages, health knowledge and perceptions of risks, intentions to change behaviour and actual behavioural changes.

Baseline and follow-up

Parties should consider adopting strategies to evaluate the impact of packaging and labelling measures both before and at regular intervals after they are implemented.

Resources

The extent and complexity of actions to evaluate the impact of tobacco product packaging and labelling measures will vary among Parties, depending on the objectives and the availability of resources and expertise.

Dissemination

Parties should consider publishing, or making available to other Parties and to the public, the results gathered from monitoring of compliance and evaluating impact.

INTERNATIONAL COOPERATION

International cooperation is essential for progress in such an important, constantly changing area as tobacco control. Several articles of the Convention provide for exchanges of knowledge and experience to promote progress in implementation, with a particular focus on the needs of developing country Parties and Parties with economies in transition. Cooperation among Parties to promote the transfer of technical, scientific and legal expertise and technology, as required by Article 22, would strengthen the implementation of Article 11 of the Convention globally. One example of such cooperation would be the provision of licences quickly, easily and without cost from Parties to other jurisdictions seeking to use their pictorial health warnings. International cooperation would also help to ensure that consistent and accurate information relating to tobacco products is provided globally.

Parties should endeavour to share legal and other expertise in countering tobacco industry arguments against packaging and labelling measures.

Parties should consider reviewing the reports of other Parties, pursuant to Article 21 of the Convention, to enhance their knowledge of international experience with respect to packaging and labelling.

Guidelines for implementation
Article 12

Guidelines for implementation of Article 12 of the WHO Framework Convention on Tobacco Control

EDUCATION, COMMUNICATION, TRAINING AND PUBLIC AWARENESS

PURPOSE, OBJECTIVES AND PRINCIPLES OF THE GUIDELINES

Purpose

The purpose of the guidelines is to assist Parties in meeting their obligations under Article 12 and other related articles of the WHO Framework Convention on Tobacco Control. The guidelines propose measures to increase the effectiveness of education, communication and training efforts that raise public awareness of matters related to tobacco control. The guidelines draw on the available research-based evidence, best practices and experience gained by Parties, to establish a high standard of accountability for treaty compliance and to assist Parties in achieving the highest attainable standard of health through education, communication and training. Parties are also encouraged to implement any necessary measures beyond those required by the Convention and its protocols or suggested in these guidelines, in accordance with Article 2.1 of the Convention.[1]

Objectives

The objectives of the guidelines are:

> (a) to identify key legislative, executive, administrative, fiscal and other measures necessary to successfully educate, communicate with and train people on the health, social, economic and environmental consequences of tobacco production,[2] consumption and exposure to tobacco smoke; and

> (b) to guide Parties in establishing an infrastructure that includes the sustainable resources required to support such measures, based on scientific evidence and/or good practice.

Guiding principles

The following guiding principles underpin the implementation of Article 12.

> (i) *The exercise of fundamental human rights and freedoms.* The duty to educate, communicate with and train people to ensure a high level of public awareness of tobacco control, the harms of tobacco

---

[1] Parties are directed to the WHO Framework Convention on Tobacco Control web site (http://www.who.int/fctc/) where further sources of information on topics covered by these guidelines are maintained.
[2] Including growing, manufacturing and marketing.

production, consumption and exposure to tobacco smoke, and the strategies and practices of the tobacco industry to undermine tobacco control efforts (as embodied in Article 12), derives from the Convention and reflects fundamental human rights and freedoms. These include, but are not limited to the right to life, the right to the highest attainable standard of health and the right to education.[3] The mandate of Article 12 is widely reflected throughout the WHO Framework Convention on Tobacco Control.[4]

(ii) *Protection from threats to fundamental rights and freedoms.* Governments should adopt and implement effective legislative, executive, administrative or other measures to protect individuals from threats to their fundamental rights and freedoms.[1,2]

(iii) *A comprehensive multisectoral approach.* Effective education, communication and public awareness programmes on the harm caused by the use of all tobacco products, including new and alternative products, and the impact these may have on vulnerable groups, as well as the strategies and practices of the tobacco industry to undermine tobacco control efforts, all call for a comprehensive multisectoral approach, as specified in Articles 4.4 and 5.2 of the Convention.

(iv) *Protection of public health policies from the tobacco industry.* The development and implementation of public health policies and programmes should be protected from commercial and other vested interests of the tobacco industry, as embodied in Article 5.3 of the Convention and elaborated in the guidelines on implementing Article 5.3, in particular guiding principle 1.

---

[3] These rights are recognized in many international legal instruments (including Articles 3 and 25 of the Universal Declaration of Human Rights, the Preamble to the Constitution of the World Health Organization, the Convention on the Rights of the Child, the Convention on the Elimination of All Forms of Discrimination against Women, and the International Covenant on Economic, Social and Cultural Rights), are formally incorporated into the Preamble of the WHO Framework Convention on Tobacco Control and are recognized in the constitutions of many countries. The right to education is specified in Article 13 of the International Covenant on Economic, Social and Cultural Rights and the United Nations Economic and Social Council General Comment No. 13 (E/C.12/1999/10).
[4] These rights are addressed in following articles of the Framework Convention: Article 2 (Relationship between this Convention and other agreements and legal instruments), Article 3 (Objective), Article 4 (Guiding principles), Article 5 (General obligations), Article 8 (Protection from exposure to tobacco smoke), Article 10 (Regulation of tobacco product disclosures), Article 11 (Packaging and labelling of tobacco products), Article 14 (Demand reduction measures concerning tobacco dependence and cessation), Article 17 (Provision of support for economically viable alternative activities), Article 18 (Protection of the environment and the health of persons), Article 19 (Liability), Article 20 (Research, surveillance and exchange of information), Article 21 (Reporting and exchange of information), and Article 22 (Cooperation in the scientific, technical and legal fields and provision of related expertise).

(v) *Research-based[5] evidence and best practices.* Research-based evidence and best practices with regard to the circumstances in each country are fundamental to the elaboration, management and implementation of education, communication and training programmes aimed at raising public awareness of tobacco-control issues. Where resources permit, such programmes should undergo rigorous pre-testing, monitoring and evaluation at local, national/federal, regional and/or international level, as outlined in Article 20 of the Convention. Where resources do not permit and where evidence is not available in a specific country, evidence collected in and shared by other countries can be a starting-point for programme development, as described in Articles 20 and 22 of the Convention.

(vi) *International cooperation.* International cooperation and mutual support are fundamental to and necessary for strengthening the capacity of Parties to elaborate, manage and implement education, communication and training programmes, as described in Articles 4.3, 5.5, 20 and 22 of the Convention. Research-based outcomes and best practices should be regularly identified, implemented and shared among Parties.

(vii) *Norm change.* It is essential to change social, environmental and cultural norms and perceptions regarding the acceptability of the consumption of tobacco products, exposure to tobacco smoke, and aspects of the growing, manufacturing, marketing and sale of tobacco and tobacco products.

(viii) *Adequacy of resources.* It is essential to ensure that adequate resources are available to sustain comprehensive, multisectoral tobacco-control education and other awareness-raising programmes, making use, where appropriate, of bilateral and multilateral funding mechanisms as set out in Articles 5.6 and 26 of the Convention.

(ix) *Communication with all people.* It is essential that every person is aware of and has access to accurate and comprehensible information on the adverse health, socioeconomic and environmental consequences of tobacco production, consumption and exposure to tobacco smoke; on the benefits of cessation of

---

[5] The term "research-based" refers to the use of rigorous, systematic, and objective methodologies to obtain reliable and valid knowledge relevant to education, communication and training activities and programmes. Specifically, such research in this case requires: (a) development of a logical, evidence-based chain of reasoning; (b) methods appropriate to the questions posed; (c) observational or experimental designs and instruments that provide reliable and generalizable findings; (d) data and analysis adequate to support findings; (e) explication of procedures and results clearly and in detail, including specification of the population to which the findings can be generalized; (f) adherence to professional norms of peer review; (g) dissemination of findings to contribute to scientific knowledge; (h) access to data for reanalysis, replication, and the opportunity to build on findings; (i) adherence to research ethics, including an unbiased approach and equipoise; and (j) independence from the commercial and other vested interests of the tobacco industry.

tobacco use and of living a tobacco-free life; and a wide range of information on the tobacco industry, as outlined in Articles 4.1 and 12 of the Convention.

(x) *Consideration of key differences.* The consideration of key differences among population groups in relation to gender, age, religion, culture, educational background, socioeconomic status, literacy and disability is of paramount importance in the development and implementation of education, communication and training programmes for tobacco control.

(xi) *Active participation of civil society.* The active participation of and partnership with civil society, as specified in Article 4.7 of the Convention, is essential to the effective implementation of these guidelines.

PROVIDING AN INFRASTRUCTURE TO RAISE PUBLIC AWARENESS

Background

Public awareness of tobacco-control issues is essential to ensure social change. Tools to raise public awareness are important means of bringing about change in the behavioural norms around tobacco consumption and exposure to tobacco smoke. Comprehensive tobacco-control programmes contain research-based tools in education, communication and training – the three pillars of public awareness.

Infrastructure to raise public awareness refers to the organizational structures and capacity needed to ensure sustained education, communication and training programmes. It provides the means and resources needed to gather knowledge, translate research results and good practices into useful and understandable messages for individual target groups, communicate the relevant messages, and then monitor the effects of these messages on knowledge, attitude and behavioural outcomes.

Building on effective national coordinating mechanisms or focal points, the infrastructure should take into account local, national/federal and regional specificities, including traditional structures, to ensure that various population groups in both urban and rural settings are reached.

Recommendation[6]

Parties should establish an infrastructure to support education, communication and training and ensure that they are used effectively to raise public awareness and promote social change, in order to prevent, reduce or eliminate tobacco consumption and exposure to tobacco smoke.

---

[6] *Recommendations* are general political and programmatic suggestions to assist Parties in implementing Article 12 of the Convention.

Action points[7]

Parties should implement the actions listed below, taking into account national circumstances, priorities and resources.

Establish a coordinating mechanism or focal points according to Article 5.2(a) of the Convention. Define its role, in order to ensure, within the overall tobacco control strategies, plans and programmes, good planning, management and adequate funding for programmes based on Article 12 of the Convention. This coordinating mechanism or focal point should play a catalytic, coordination, and facilitation role in the delivery of tobacco-related education, communication and training programmes, by setting specific objectives, and then monitoring and evaluating their progress and outcomes.

Specify the people, bodies or entities responsible for tobacco-control education, communication and training, and define the role of governmental and nongovernmental bodies involved, to ensure cooperation within and between governments (including relevant authorities, such as ministries of education and science, health and consumer protection, finance and customs, economy and technology).

Define the role of programmes based on Article 12 of the Convention in relation to other public health programmes.

Establish action plans for the implementation of education, communication and training activities within a comprehensive tobacco-control programme.[8]

Ensure legitimacy and formal recognition of programmes based on Article 12 of the Convention through broad consultation among implementing bodies or entities and enforcing authorities. Ensure that the programme is research-based, that it uses regular situation analysis and assessment to determine needs and resources, and that it provides for mid-course correction if its objectives are not being met. This includes, but is not limited to: delineating the current status of tobacco-control research and identifying individuals and institutions engaged in research to determine local expertise; and identifying areas where gaps in research exist to determine the allocation of technical assistance and resources.[9]

Provide adequate human, material and financial resources to establish and sustain the programme at local, national/federal, regional and international levels, possibly using technical experts to design and execute the programme. To ensure sustainability of the programme, use existing funding sources and explore other potential sources, in accordance with Article 26 of the Convention. Potential funding mechanisms include but are not limited to raising tobacco excise taxes and introducing dedicated taxes (e.g. earmarking), licensing fees

---

[7] *Action points* are measurable objectives, practices and undertakings consistent with the recommendations. They are the proposed means of attaining the successful implementation of the recommendations.
[8] See Appendix 1 for an indicative list of items to cover in an action plan.
[9] See Appendix 2 for an indicative list of research-based strategies and programmes.

and other taxation schemes. The establishment of special foundations for tobacco-control education, communication and/or training are other potential funding mechanisms. All potential funding mechanisms must be protected against interference by the tobacco industry in accordance with the principles laid down in Article 5.3 of the Convention and its guidelines.

Provide cost-effective logistic and management support to tobacco-control programmes.

Ensure that new and developing tobacco-control organizations receive and use appropriate research-based training, training in strategic planning and technical assistance to carry out their missions and achieve sustainability.

Ensure that local, national/federal, regional and international data are collected to build a tobacco-control database or establish a central repository of research results, and ensure that the public has access to these data.

RUNNING EFFECTIVE EDUCATION, COMMUNICATION AND TRAINING PROGRAMMES

Background

Article 12 of the Convention calls for the use of all available communication tools to promote and strengthen public awareness of tobacco-control issues. Specific guidance on education, communication and training measures concerning tobacco dependence and cessation is suggested in the guidelines on Article 14.

Education, communication and training are the means of raising public awareness and achieving social change on tobacco use and exposure to tobacco smoke. To achieve the highest level of attainable health in all populations, social norms should provide enabling environments which protect against exposure to tobacco smoke, promote tobacco-free lifestyles, help tobacco users to quit tobacco use and prevent others, particularly young people, from starting.

In tobacco control, **education** comprises a continuum of teaching and learning about tobacco which empowers people to make voluntary decisions, modify their behaviour and change social conditions in ways that enhance health.

In tobacco control, **communication** is essential to change attitudes about tobacco production, manufacture, marketing, consumption and exposure to tobacco smoke, discourage tobacco use, curb smoking initiation, and encourage cessation, as well as being necessary for effective community mobilization towards providing enabling environments and achieving sustainable social change.

In tobacco control, **training** describes the process of building and sustaining the necessary capacity for a comprehensive tobacco-control programme through attaining vocational or practical skills and knowledge that relate to specific core competencies.

Promotion of social and environmental change refers to strategies, events or actions that promote visible and sustained changes in social and environmental norms and behaviour patterns within social groups. It is an important means of bringing about change in the behavioural norms around tobacco production, consumption and exposure to tobacco smoke.

Recommendation

Parties should use all available means to raise awareness, provide enabling environments and facilitate behavioural and social change through sustained education, communication and training.

Action points

Parties should implement the actions listed below, taking into account national circumstances, priorities and resources.

General

When planning, implementing and evaluating education, communication, training and other public-awareness programmes, develop a coordinated research-based approach.[10]

Ensure inclusiveness of priority populations, consider and address key differences among population groups.[11] Interventions should include effective messages and ensure that everyone is reached without discrimination or unequal allocation of resources. Special attention should be paid to those most affected by marketing and rising tobacco use, such as young people, particularly young women, who are targeted as "replacement smokers", as well as frequently neglected groups such as those who are illiterate, uneducated or undereducated, the poor, and people with disabilities. In addition, measures could be taken to raise awareness among parents, teachers, educators and pregnant women.

Ensure that the adverse health, socioeconomic and environmental consequences of tobacco production and consumption, of exposure to tobacco smoke, and the strategies and practices of the tobacco industry to undermine tobacco control efforts are communicated as widely as possible, and that the benefits of cessation of tobacco use and of a tobacco-free life are highlighted.[12]

Combine formative research, process evaluation and outcome evaluation to ensure the greatest possible likelihood that the programmes will effectively build knowledge and awareness, and change attitudes and behaviours as intended. Such research and evaluation should be as current as possible and evidence-based as far as possible, but not limit innovative approaches.

Identify and implement best practices at the local, national/federal and regional levels, and facilitate international cooperation through sharing

---

[10] See Appendix 2 for an indicative list of research-based strategies and programmes.
[11] In accordance with guiding principle (x).
[12] See Appendix 3 for an indicative list of areas to cover.

research-based outcomes and best practices as specified in Article 22 of the Convention.

Introduce measures to ensure that entities involved in education, communication and training, and related research, including but not limited to academia, professional associations and governmental agencies, fully respect the principles laid down in Article 5.3 of the Convention and its guidelines, and thus do not accept any direct or indirect tobacco industry funding.

Consumption, tobacco advertising, promotion and sponsorship, and sales of tobacco products should be banned on premises used for educational or training purposes in order to complement tobacco-free messages, in accordance with Articles 8 and 13 of the Convention and the guidelines on their implementation.

Personnel involved in education, training and communication should avoid using tobacco because:

> (a) they are role models and by using tobacco, they undermine public health messages about its effect on health; and

> (b) it is important to reduce the social acceptability of tobacco use and personnel involved in education, training and communication should set a good example in this respect.

Public education and communication activities

Develop and implement public education programmes at different levels, following a life-course approach.[13]

Develop or adapt existing communication tools and activities, such as campaigns, according to the needs, knowledge, attitudes and behaviours of each target population, particularly aiming to ensure taking into account that they:

> (a) are appropriate to the target audience;

> (b) are of high frequency/long duration;

> (c) contain refreshed and targeted messages;

> (d) use a variety of methods and media vehicles;[14]

> (e) use lessons learnt from other successful campaigns; and

> (f) use integrated evaluation.

Communicate messages that are relevant, comprehensible, interesting, realistic, accurate, persuasive and empowering, while taking into account the

---

[13] See Appendix 4 for an indicative list of venues for educational programmes.
[14] See Appendix 5 for an indicative list of methods and media vehicles.

effectiveness of key messages and the results of sound scientific research, where available. Acknowledge the potential role of both negative and positive messages by including a wide range of relevant information.[15]

Identify the most appropriate media to reach the intended audience, based on reach and relevance to the target groups. The opportunities and potential risks of using new and innovative communication and marketing vehicles, as well as new technologies, should be investigated and applied or avoided accordingly.

Consider supplementing mass media with community-based (including traditional) communication approaches, which may, for example, be used to reach low-income urban and rural populations in developing countries.

Maximize the coverage of education and communication campaigns by targeting vulnerable populations, including low-income and rural populations. Outreach can also be increased by encouraging and supporting nongovernmental organizations and other members of civil society active in the field of tobacco control, and not affiliated with the tobacco industry, to complement governmental programmes through joint and/or independent educational activities and communication campaigns. Campaigns by, and with the participation of, civil society could be integrated into existing community education and mobilization programmes.

Monitor and evaluate the outcomes of public education and communication interventions in different target groups and take key differences, such as gender, cultural and educational background, age, and literacy into account in such monitoring and evaluation work. Identify effective research-based key messages for each of the target groups and use them to improve the responsiveness of programmes to each group, in particular those with the greatest needs.

Training[16]

Identify training needs at the local, national/federal, regional and international levels, design a relevant training plan and select, implement and evaluate the resulting training programmes in different settings, focusing on the various needs. To increase reach and relevance, training programmes may follow the concept of place, people and practice, covering different environmental settings (e.g. rural, urban, and suburban), educational facilities (e.g. in formal, non-formal, and continuous education), and health-care providers (e.g. hospitals, primary health-care facilities and traditional healers) and so on.

Provide training for key professionals, as appropriate, including: physicians and other health workers; community workers; social workers; media professionals; educators; decision-makers; traditional communicators; healers (traditional medical or spiritual practitioners); religious and spiritual counsellors; administrators and fiscal, customs and justice officials; tobacco growers/workers; and other concerned persons.

---

[15] See Appendix 3 for an indicative list of information to cover in communication and education campaigns.
[16] Further recommendations covering training on demand-reduction measures are given in the draft guidelines on implementation of Article 14 (document FCTC/COP/4/8).

Design a research-based training plan to ensure continued training of the relevant groups in the required competencies, including knowledge of effective tobacco-control measures and the vocational or practical skills needed to achieve them. Training programmes should include information about the strategies and practices of the tobacco industry to undermine tobacco-control efforts.

Identify the appropriate training methods for each target group,[17] including the integration of novel approaches into training programmes.[18]

Integrate the different aspects of tobacco control, including the adverse health, social, economic, and environmental consequences of tobacco production and consumption, as well as information on new tobacco products, into relevant curricula of universities, professional schools and other relevant vocational teaching institutions. Advance the introduction of tobacco-control education or training into the licensing requirements for relevant professions, as well as into requirements for continuous professional development.

Involve both practitioners and academic experts in capacity building and the development of research-based training tools, including professional associations, student organizations, and organizations active in formal and non-formal education and training. Identify influential groups and role models, such as government focal point staff, policy-makers, administrators, health professionals, media professionals or others who can contribute to training activities.

Monitor and evaluate the outcomes of training programmes at the local, national/federal, regional and international levels to identify the most appropriate training methods to be used for each target group.[19]

Introduce and sustain budgetary provisions to meet the requirements for implementing training curricula and updating them periodically.

INVOLVING CIVIL SOCIETY

Background

The Preamble and Article 4.7 of the Convention emphasize the contribution of nongovernmental organizations and other members of civil society. The participation of civil society[20] is of vital importance to national and international tobacco-control efforts. Vigilance must be exercised to ensure they are not affiliated with the tobacco industry, in accordance with the guidelines on Article 5.3 of the Convention.

---

[17] See Appendix 6 for an indicative list of types of training (including examples of training for specific target groups).
[18] See Appendix 7 for an indicative list of different types of novel approaches.
[19] See Appendix 8 for an indicative list of different approaches to training methods for specific target groups.
[20] See Appendix 9 for an indicative list of members of civil society to consider actively involving in education, communication, training and public awareness programmes.

Recommendation

Parties should actively involve members of civil society, in different phases such as planning, developing, implementing, monitoring and evaluating education, communication and training programmes.

Parties should restrict their collaboration to members of civil society not affiliated with the tobacco industry.[21]

Action points

Parties should implement the actions listed below, taking into account national circumstances, priorities and resources.

Regularly consult, cooperate and form effective partnerships with civil society involved in tobacco control education, communication and training, including but not limited to bodies representing key target groups.

Ensure civil society involvement in and collaboration with the governmental coordinating mechanism or focal point in planning, developing, implementing, monitoring and evaluating tobacco control education, communication and training programmes, including physical representation.

Work with civil society to create a climate of attitude that:

    (a) engenders public and political support for action to control tobacco use;

    (b) supports the government in its tobacco-control efforts;

    (c) identifies legislative priorities and helps develop and enforce legislative measures;

    (d) makes the case that tobacco-control measures are reasonable and effective;

    (e) increases awareness of tobacco industry interference; and

    (f) provides a powerful and respectable public image for education, communication, training and awareness campaigns.

Identify key professionals, including but not limited to health professionals, teachers, journalists and other media professionals, and involve them as role models and agents of change in education, communication and training.

Build and strengthen tobacco-control movements and support effective tobacco-control alliances, for example by providing seed grants to support civil society groups and coalitions for tobacco control.

---

[21] In accordance with the guidelines on Article 5.3 of the Framework Convention, this includes the tobacco industry itself as well as organizations and individuals that work to further the interests of the tobacco industry.

ENSURING WIDE ACCESS TO INFORMATION ON THE TOBACCO INDUSTRY[22]

Background

Evidence demonstrates that tobacco companies use a wide range of tactics to interfere with tobacco control. Such strategies include direct and indirect political lobbying and campaign contributions, financing of research, attempts to affect the course of regulatory and policy machinery and engaging in so-called "corporate social responsibility" initiatives as part of public relations campaigns. The implementation guidelines on Article 5.3 of the Convention, especially recommendation 5.5, outline the information that Parties should require from the tobacco industry and those working to further its interests. To ensure that the obligations under Article 12 of the Convention are met, the public needs to have access to this information and all programmes should be protected from commercial and other vested interests of the tobacco industry (as described in Article 5.3).

Recommendation

Parties should ensure that the public has free and universal access to accurate and truthful information on the strategies and activities of the tobacco industry[23] and its products,1 as appropriate, and that education, communication, training and public awareness programmes include a wide range of information on the tobacco industry as they require and in accordance with Articles 12(c) and 20.4(c) of the Convention.

Action points

Parties should implement the actions listed below, taking into account national circumstances, priorities and resources.

Adopt and implement effective measures that require the tobacco industry to be accountable and to provide accurate and transparent information in accordance with Article 12(c) and the implementing guidelines on Articles 5.3, 9, 10, 11 and 13 of the Convention.

Provide public access to all information relevant to the strategies and activities of the tobacco industry, through such means as publicly accessible databases, monitoring instruments and research-based literature, and by publicizing trustworthy sources of information on the tobacco industry.

Consider putting in place education programmes, communication campaigns and training courses that can effectively inform and educate the public and all branches of government about:

> (a) tobacco industry interference with activities related to education, communication and training, such as tobacco industry funded or co-funded youth prevention programmes, which have been demonstrated

---

[22] In accordance with Articles 9 and 10 of the Convention and the draft implementation guidelines on these articles (document FCTC/COP/4/6).
[23] See the implementation guidelines on Article 5.3, recommendation 5.2.

to be ineffective and even counterproductive, and have been publicly disapproved by the World Health Organization; and

(b) tobacco industry interference with Parties' tobacco-control policies.[24] Consider ways to build sufficient capacity to enable effective monitoring and surveillance of the tobacco industry and its products, by training researchers and other relevant professionals, and by providing easy public access to relevant data on the tobacco industry and its products, as required in Article 12(c) of the Convention.

Develop and implement communication tools to facilitate public access to a wide range of information on the tobacco industry and its products.[25] Depending on cultural appropriateness, reach and accessibility, such communication tools could include:

(a) public repositories on the tobacco industry, such as the Legacy Tobacco Industry Documents Library;[26] and

(b) counter-advertising campaigns using the media and/or relevant forms of modern technology.

STRENGTHENING INTERNATIONAL COOPERATION

Background

International collaboration, mutual support and sharing of information, knowledge and relevant technical capacity are vitally important to strengthen Parties' capacities to meet their obligations under Article 12 of the Convention and to successfully counter the adverse health, socioeconomic and environmental consequences of tobacco production, consumption and exposure to tobacco smoke. The duty to cooperate in the development of effective measures, procedures and guidelines for implementation of the Convention, to cooperate with international and regional organizations and to use bilateral and multilateral funding mechanisms, derives from Articles 4.3, 5.4, 5.5, 20, 21 and 22 of the Convention.

Recommendation

Parties should collaborate at the international level to raise global public awareness.

Action points

Parties should implement the actions listed below, taking into account national circumstances, priorities and resources.

Make available to other Parties strategies, data and experiences on planned and/or implemented public education programmes, communication campaigns

---
[24] As specified in recommendations 1.1 and 1.2 of the implementation guidelines on Article 5.3 of the Convention.
[25] In accordance with recommendation 5.5 of the guidelines on Article 5.3 of the Convention.
[26] See http://legacy.library.ucsf.edu/.

and training efforts, impart practical skills and core competencies, and share best practices. Where appropriate, use international reporting mechanisms, such as the regular reporting instruments of the Convention on implementation, and take advantage of bilateral and multilateral contacts.

Use the multisectoral approach of the Convention. Raise awareness of its implementation in relevant international organizations, platforms and civil society to ensure that raising awareness of the Convention is not confined to tobacco-control meetings and the health sector.

MONITORING OF IMPLEMENTATION AND REVISION OF THE GUIDELINES

Background

Monitoring and evaluation of the implementation of Article 12 of the Convention are essential to ensuring that adequate means are employed to raise public awareness. Monitoring and evaluation at both national and international levels optimize the gains in implementation of the Convention. At country level, progress made becomes measurable and best practices can be identified to make effective use of resources. At the international level, the sharing of experiences and information allows Parties to adapt and improve their strategies and actions to have a broader impact on public awareness.

Recommendations

Parties should monitor, evaluate and revise their communication, education and training measures nationally and internationally to meet their obligations under the Convention, to enable comparisons and observe any trends.

Parties reporting via the existing reporting instrument of the Convention should provide information on education, communication, training and raising public awareness.

Parties should make use of the Convention and its monitoring instruments to raise awareness on its implementation, for example by communicating success stories and addressing gaps in the implementation of Article 12 of the Convention. Parties could also consider carrying out activities to raise the profile of the Convention as an effective international tobacco control strategy.

Action points

Parties should implement the actions listed below, taking into account national circumstances, priorities and resources.

Ensure that programmes in education, communication, and training are regularly monitored and evaluated, and the results made available for comparison and used for programme improvement.

Determine the needs, formulate measurable objectives and identify the resources required to implement actions based on these guidelines, and identify key indicators such as relevance, persuasion or behaviour change to assess the progress for each objective and achievement of outcomes.

Routinely collect data on the implementation of Article 12 of the Convention through surveys and other relevant research undertaken by government, nongovernmental organizations, or any other relevant entities.

Use the reporting instrument of the Convention to capture and share information on the policies adopted and any other measures taken in the implementation of Article 12.[27]

KEY MESSAGES

With respect to the implementation of Article 12 of the WHO Framework Convention on Tobacco Control, Parties should:

(a) establish an infrastructure and build capacity to support education, communication and training, thereby raising public awareness and promoting social change;

(b) use all available means to raise awareness, provide enabling environments and facilitate behavioural and social change;

(c) actively involve civil society in relevant phases of public awareness programmes;

(d) ensure that education, communication, and training programmes include a wide range of information on the tobacco industry, its strategies and its products;

(e) collaborate at the international level to raise global public awareness;

(f) monitor, evaluate and revise education, communication and training measures nationally and internationally to enable comparisons and observe any trends;

(g) provide information on education, communication, and training via the existing reporting instrument of the Convention to monitor its implementation; and

(h) make use of the WHO Framework Convention on Tobacco Control and its monitoring instruments to raise awareness on its implementation and consider carrying out activities to raise the profile of the Convention as an effective international tobacco control strategy.

---

[27] See Appendix 10 for an indicative list of useful information to consider in reporting at the international level.

APPENDIX 1

Indicative (non-exhaustive) checklist for an action plan for the implementation of education, communication and training activities within a comprehensive tobacco-control programme

- State the vision
- Develop a mission statement
- Formulate goals and objectives
- Select strategies and expected results for each objective
- Prepare a budget plan
- Indicate who is responsible for each activity
- Set target dates and determine the resources required
- Identify progress indicators to enable measurement of the effectiveness of implementation
- Monitor and evaluate implementation and outcomes
- Disseminate results to people, bodies or entities responsible for tobacco-control education, communication and training[28]

APPENDIX 2

Indicative (non-exhaustive) checklist for research-based strategies and programmes

- Conduct regular situation analyses and assessments of needs
- Identify priority target groups
- Determine behavioural change objectives
- Identify indicators
- Develop and pre-test messages
- Select intervention methods
- Obtain financing
- Identify partners
- Monitor and evaluate
- Coordinate among governmental and related bodies
- Disseminate results, including through earned media

APPENDIX 3

Indicative (non-exhaustive) list of areas to cover in education, communication and training programmes

- The benefits of a tobacco-free life and cessation of tobacco use.

---

[28] As indicated under Action Points in "Providing an infrastructure to raise public awareness".

- The health effects of tobacco agriculture, production, consumption and exposure to tobacco smoke, including but not limited to epidemiological data on the contribution of tobacco to morbidity and mortality and information on novel tobacco products.
- The health, social, environmental and economic costs and consequences of tobacco agriculture, production and consumption, including health-care costs, lost productivity, premature deaths, environmental impact, and contribution to poverty.
- Local, national/federal, regional and international policies and reports related to tobacco and tobacco control, including but not limited to the Convention and its implementation guidelines.
- Information on the strategies and activities of the tobacco industry to undermine tobacco-control efforts, and on the ineffectiveness of activities related to tobacco control funded by the tobacco industry, e.g. public-awareness campaigns aimed at youth.
- Techniques for effective behaviour support (counselling skills) for tobacco dependence.

APPENDIX 4

Indicative (non-exhaustive) list of venues for educational programmes

- Homes
- Schools and school-like environments, including primary and secondary schools, colleges and universities, as well as continuous education and lifelong-learning programmes
- Sports, recreation and leisure facilities
- Workplaces
- Health-care facilities
- Communities
- Reformative and rehabilitative facilities

APPENDIX 5

Indicative (non-exhaustive) list of appropriate methods and media vehicles

Methods include counter-marketing by means of:

- paid advertising;
- media placements; and
- earned media including but not limited to events which capture the attention of journalists and the public.

Media vehicles include:

- television;
- radio;
- newspapers;
- magazines;
- billboards; and
- electronic media, e.g. text messages, e-mail, web sites, blogs, social networks, etc.

APPENDIX 6

Indicative (non-exhaustive) list of types of training

- Orientation training and interaction (with survivors of tobacco-related diseases and disability)
- Public speaking skills (for people talking to news media and other organizations about tobacco control)
- Media advocacy skills and media training
- Networking training
- Campaign planning
- Evaluation training
- Peer education
- Training on the negative impacts of tobacco and cost–effectiveness of tobacco-control interventions
- News media staff training on tobacco-control issues
- Capacity building on tobacco industry interference in school-based training programmes and so-called youth smoking prevention programmes
- Social media training

APPENDIX 7

Indicative (non-exhaustive) list of types of novel approaches

- E-learning and web-based approaches
- Peer education
- Train-the-trainer models
- Cross-training opportunities through existing programmes, such as reproductive health programmes (including those on HIV/AIDS), disease-management programmes (e.g. DOTS), substance-abuse prevention programmes (e.g. those aimed at alcohol or illicit drugs) or environmental protection programmes

APPENDIX 8

Indicative (non-exhaustive) list of different approaches of training methods for specific target groups

Monitoring data should distinguish, inter alia, between the different training methods used according to:

- the place of the intervention (settings such as educational facilities, workplaces, and health-care facilities);
- the people performing the intervention (providers, such as health workers, social workers, educators, and counsellors); and
- the practice involved (method used to reach the target audience, such as radio, skits, and lectures).

APPENDIX 9

Indicative (non-exhaustive) list of members of civil society to consider actively involving in education, communication, training and public awareness programmes

- Nongovernmental organizations, including women's, youth, environmental and consumer groups
- Foundations
- Professional organizations
- Private agencies
- Academia
- Teaching and training institutions
- Health-care institutions

APPENDIX 10

Indicative (non-exhaustive) list of useful information to consider in reporting at the international level

- Results of monitoring and evaluating of education, communication, training and public-awareness interventions
- Outcomes of evaluations undertaken at the national level
- The most appropriate strategies identified in each country
- The major challenges faced
- The activities of the tobacco industry

Guidelines for implementation
Article 13

Guidelines for implementation of Article 13 of the WHO Framework Convention on Tobacco Control

TOBACCO ADVERTISING, PROMOTION AND SPONSORSHIP

PURPOSE AND OBJECTIVES

The purpose of these guidelines is to assist Parties in meeting their obligations under Article 13 of the WHO Framework Convention on Tobacco Control. They draw on the best available evidence and the experience of Parties that have successfully implemented effective measures against tobacco advertising, promotion and sponsorship. They give Parties guidance for introducing and enforcing a comprehensive ban on tobacco advertising, promotion and sponsorship or, for those Parties that are not in a position to undertake a comprehensive ban owing to their constitutions or constitutional principles, for applying restrictions on tobacco advertising, promotion and sponsorship that are as comprehensive as possible.

These guidelines provide guidance on the best ways to implement Article 13 of the Convention in order to eliminate tobacco advertising, promotion and sponsorship effectively at both domestic and international levels.

The following principles apply:

(a) It is well documented that tobacco advertising, promotion and sponsorship increase tobacco use and that comprehensive bans on tobacco advertising, promotion and sponsorship decrease tobacco use.

(b) An effective ban on tobacco advertising, promotion and sponsorship should, as recognized by Parties to the Convention in Articles 13.1 and 13.2, be *comprehensive* and applicable to *all* tobacco advertising, promotion and sponsorship.

(c) According to the definitions in Article 1 of the Convention, a comprehensive ban on all tobacco advertising, promotion and sponsorship applies to *all* forms of *commercial communication, recommendation or action* and all forms of *contribution* to any event, activity or individual with the *aim, effect, or likely effect* of promoting a tobacco product or tobacco use either *directly or indirectly*.

(d) A comprehensive ban on tobacco advertising, promotion and sponsorship should include *cross-border advertising, promotion and sponsorship*. This includes both out-flowing advertising, promotion and sponsorship (originating from a Party's territory) and in-flowing advertising, promotion and sponsorship (entering a Party's territory).

(e) To be effective, a comprehensive ban should address *all persons or entities* involved in the production, placement and/or dissemination of tobacco advertising, promotion and sponsorship.

(f) Effective *monitoring, enforcement and sanctions* supported and facilitated by strong *public education and community awareness programmes* are essential for implementation of a comprehensive ban on tobacco advertising, promotion and sponsorship.

(g) *Civil society* has a central role in building support for, developing and ensuring compliance with laws addressing tobacco advertising, promotion and sponsorship, and it should be included as an active partner in this process.

(h) Effective *international cooperation* is fundamental to the elimination of both domestic and cross-border tobacco advertising, promotion and sponsorship.

SCOPE OF A COMPREHENSIVE BAN

The scope of a comprehensive ban on tobacco advertising, promotion and sponsorship is outlined in general terms in subsection "Overview" below, while the subsections from "Retail sale and display" to "Communication within the tobacco trade" inclusive address aspects that could pose special challenges for regulators in introducing a comprehensive ban.

Overview

A ban on tobacco advertising, promotion and sponsorship is effective only if it has a broad scope. Contemporary marketing communication involves an integrated approach to advertising and promoting the purchase and sale of goods, including direct marketing, public relations, sales promotion, personal selling and online interactive marketing methods. If only certain forms of direct tobacco advertising are prohibited, the tobacco industry inevitably shifts its expenditure to other advertising, promotion and sponsorship strategies, using creative, indirect ways to promote tobacco products and tobacco use, especially among young people.

Therefore, the effect of a partial advertising ban on tobacco consumption is limited. This is recognized in Article 13 of the Convention, which lays down the basic obligation to ban tobacco advertising, promotion and sponsorship. According to Article 13.1 of the Convention, "Parties recognize that a comprehensive ban on advertising, promotion and sponsorship would reduce the consumption of tobacco products".

To implement the comprehensive ban laid down in Articles 13.1 and 13.2 of the Convention, Parties should ban advertising, promotion and sponsorship as defined in Article 1(c) and (g) of the Convention. Article 1(c) defines "tobacco advertising and promotion" as "any form of commercial communication, recommendation or action with the aim, effect or likely effect of promoting a tobacco product or tobacco use either directly or indirectly". Article 1(g) defines "tobacco sponsorship" as "any form of contribution to any event, activity or individual with the aim, effect or likely effect of promoting a tobacco product or tobacco use either directly or indirectly".

It is important to note that both "tobacco advertising and promotion" and "tobacco sponsorship" cover promotion not only of particular tobacco products but also of tobacco use generally; not only acts with a promotional aim but also acts that have a promotional effect or are likely to have a promotional effect; and not only direct promotion but also indirect promotion. "Tobacco advertising and promotion" is not restricted to "communications", but also includes "recommendations" and "actions", which should cover at least the following categories: (a) various sales and/or distribution arrangements[9]; (b) hidden forms of advertising or promotion, such as insertion of tobacco products or tobacco use in various media contents; (c) association of tobacco products with events or with other products in various ways; (d) promotional packaging and product design features; and (e) production and distribution of items such as sweets and toys or other products that resemble cigarettes or other tobacco products.[1] It is also important to note that the definition of "tobacco sponsorship" covers "any form of contribution", financial or otherwise, regardless of how or whether that contribution is acknowledged or publicized.

Promotional effects, both direct and indirect, may be brought about by the use of words, designs, images, sounds and colours, including brand names, trademarks, logos, names of tobacco manufacturers or importers, and colours or schemes of colours associated with tobacco products, manufacturers or importers, or by the use of a part or parts of words, designs, images and colours. Promotion of tobacco companies themselves (sometimes referred to as corporate promotion) is a form of promotion of tobacco products or tobacco use, even without the presentation of brand names or trademarks. Advertising, including display and sponsorship of smoking accessories such as cigarette papers, filters and equipment for rolling cigarettes, as well as imitations of tobacco products, may also have the effect of promoting tobacco products or tobacco use.

Legislation should avoid providing lists of prohibited activities that are, or could be understood to be, exhaustive. While it is often useful to provide examples of prohibited activities, when legislation does so, it should make clear that they are only examples and do not cover the full range of prohibited

---

[1] For instance, incentive schemes for retailers, display at points of sale, lotteries, free gifts, free samples, discounts, competitions (whether the purchase of tobacco products is required or not) and incentive promotions or loyalty schemes, e.g. redeemable coupons provided with purchase of tobacco products.

activities. This can be made clear by using terms like "including but not limited to" or catch-all phrases such as "or any other form of tobacco advertising, promotion or sponsorship".

An indicative (non-exhaustive) list of forms of advertising, promotion and sponsorship that fall under the ban in Article 13 of the Convention is attached in the appendix to these guidelines.

Recommendation

A comprehensive ban on tobacco advertising, promotion and sponsorship, should cover:

- all advertising and promotion, as well as sponsorship, without exemption;
- direct and indirect advertising, promotion and sponsorship;
- acts that aim at promotion and acts that have or are likely to have a promotional effect;
- promotion of tobacco products and the use of tobacco;
- commercial communications and commercial recommendations and actions;
- contribution of any kind to any event, activity or individual;
- advertising and promotion of tobacco brand names and all corporate promotion; and
- traditional media (print, television and radio) and all media platforms, including Internet, mobile telephones and other new technologies as well as films.

Retail sale and display

Display of tobacco products at points of sale in itself constitutes advertising and promotion. Display of products is a key means of promoting tobacco products and tobacco use, including by stimulating impulse purchases of tobacco products, giving the impression that tobacco use is socially acceptable and making it harder for tobacco users to quit. Young people are particularly vulnerable to the promotional effects of product display.

To ensure that points of sale of tobacco products do not have any promotional elements, Parties should introduce a total ban on any display and on the visibility of tobacco products at points of sale, including fixed retail outlets and street vendors. Only the textual listing of products and their prices, without any promotional elements, would be allowed. As for all aspects of Article 13

---

[2] This text reflects the spirit of Article 16.1 of the Convention, which obliges Parties to "adopt and implement effective legislative, executive, administrative or other measures at the appropriate government level to prohibit sales of tobacco products to persons under the age set by domestic law, national law or eighteen. These measures may include […] (c) prohibiting the manufacture and sale of sweets, snacks, toys or any other object in the form of tobacco products which appeal to minors".

of the Convention, the ban should also apply in ferries, airplanes, ports and airports.

Vending machines should be banned because they constitute by their very presence a means of advertising or promotion under the terms of the Convention.[3]

Recommendation
Display and visibility of tobacco products at points of sale constitutes advertising and promotion and should therefore be banned. Vending machines should be banned because they constitute, by their very presence, a means of advertising and promotion.

Packaging and product features[4]

Packaging is an important element of advertising and promotion. Tobacco pack or product features are used in various ways to attract consumers, to promote products and to cultivate and promote brand identity, for example by using logos, colours, fonts, pictures, shapes and materials on or in packs or on individual cigarettes or other tobacco products.

The effect of advertising or promotion on packaging can be eliminated by requiring plain packaging: black and white or two other contrasting colours, as prescribed by national authorities; nothing other than a brand name, a product name and/or manufacturer's name, contact details and the quantity of product in the packaging, without any logos or other features apart from health warnings, tax stamps and other government-mandated information or markings; prescribed font style and size; and standardized shape, size and materials. There should be no advertising or promotion inside or attached to the package or on individual cigarettes or other tobacco products.

If plain packaging is not yet mandated, the restriction should cover as many as possible of the design features that make tobacco products more attractive to consumers such as animal or other figures, "fun" phrases, coloured cigarette papers, attractive smells, novelty or seasonal packs.

Recommendation
Packaging and product design are important elements of advertising and promotion. Parties should consider adopting plain packaging requirements to eliminate the effects of advertising or promotion on packaging. Packaging,

---

[3] Banning vending machines because they amount to advertising or promotion complements the provisions of Article 16 of the Convention on protecting minors. The possible measures described in Article 16.1 include "ensuring that tobacco vending machines under [each Party's] jurisdiction are not accessible to minors and do not promote sale of tobacco products to minors"; and Article 16.5 stipulates that "… a Party may, by means of a binding written declaration, indicate its commitment to prohibit the introduction of tobacco vending machines within its jurisdiction or, as appropriate, to a total ban on tobacco vending machines".

[4] See also the guidelines for implementation of Article 11 of the Convention, which address plain packaging with regard to health warnings and misleading information.

individual cigarettes or other tobacco products should carry no advertising or promotion, including design features that make products attractive.

Internet sales

Internet sales of tobacco inherently involve advertising and promotion as defined in the Convention. The problem is not only limited to advertising and promotion but also includes sales to minors, tax evasion and illicit trade.

The most direct way of avoiding tobacco advertising or promotion on the Internet is to ban tobacco sales on the Internet.[5] The ban should apply not only to entities that sell the products but also to others, including credit card companies that facilitate payment and postal or delivery services for the products.

To the extent that Internet sales are not yet banned, restrictions should be imposed, allowing only textual listing of products with prices, with no pictures or promotion features (e.g. any references to low prices).

Given the covert nature of tobacco advertising and promotion on the Internet and the difficulty of identifying and reaching wrongdoers, special domestic resources are needed to make these measures operational. Measures recommended in decision FCTC/COP3(14) to eliminate cross-border tobacco advertising, promotion and sponsorship, in particular identifying contact points and dealing with notifications from other Parties, would help to ensure that domestic enforcement efforts are not undermined.

Recommendation

Internet sales of tobacco should be banned as they inherently involve tobacco advertising and promotion.

Brand stretching and brand sharing

"Brand stretching" occurs when a tobacco brand name, emblem, trademark, logo or trade insignia or any other distinctive feature (including distinctive colour combinations) is connected with a non-tobacco product or service in such a way that the tobacco product and the non-tobacco product or service are likely to be associated.

"Brand sharing" occurs when a brand name, emblem, trademark, logo or trade insignia or any other distinctive feature (including distinctive colour combinations) on a non-tobacco product or service is connected with a tobacco product or tobacco company in such a way that the tobacco product or company and the non-tobacco product or service are likely to be associated.

---

[5] Options for regulating Internet sales are being discussed by the Intergovernmental Negotiating Body on a Protocol on Illicit Trade in Tobacco Products.

"Brand stretching" and "brand sharing" should be regarded as tobacco advertising and promotion in so far as they have the aim, effect or likely effect of promoting a tobacco product or tobacco use either directly or indirectly.

Recommendation

Parties should ban "brand stretching" and "brand sharing", as they are means of tobacco advertising and promotion.

Corporate social responsibility[6]

It is increasingly common for tobacco companies to seek to portray themselves as good corporate citizens by making contributions to deserving causes or by otherwise promoting "socially responsible" elements of their business practices.

Some tobacco companies make financial or in-kind contributions to organizations, such as community, health, welfare or environmental organizations, either directly or through other entities. Such contributions fall within the definition of tobacco sponsorship in Article 1(g) of the Convention and should be prohibited as part of a comprehensive ban, because the aim, effect or likely effect of such a contribution is to promote a tobacco product or tobacco use either directly or indirectly.

Tobacco companies may also seek to engage in "socially responsible" business practices (such as good employee–employer relations or environmental stewardship), which do not involve contributions to other parties. Promotion to the public of such otherwise commendable activities should be prohibited, as their aim, effect or likely effect is to promote a tobacco product or tobacco use either directly or indirectly. Public dissemination of such information should be prohibited, except for the purposes of required corporate reporting (such as annual reports) or necessary business administration (e.g. for recruitment purposes and communications with suppliers).

Tobacco industry public education campaigns, such as "youth smoking prevention campaigns" should be prohibited on the basis that they involve "contributions" when implemented by other parties or represent corporate promotion if conducted by the industry itself.

Recommendation

The Parties should ban contributions from tobacco companies to any other entity for "socially responsible causes", as this is a form of sponsorship. Publicity given to "socially responsible" business practices of the tobacco industry should be banned, as it constitutes advertising and promotion.

---

[6] The guidelines on Article 5.3 of the Convention, elaborated by a working group established by the Conference of the Parties, address this subject from the perspective of protecting public health policies with respect to tobacco control from commercial and other vested interests of the tobacco industry

Legitimate expression

Implementation of a comprehensive ban on tobacco advertising, promotion and sponsorship should not prevent legitimate journalistic, artistic or academic expression or legitimate social or political commentary. Examples include news images with coincidental tobacco-related content in the background, the depiction of historical personalities or presentation of views on regulation or policy. Nevertheless, appropriate warnings or disclaimers may be required.

In some cases, journalistic, artistic or academic expression or social or political commentary may contain elements that are not justified for editorial, artistic, academic, social or political reasons and must be regarded as advertising, promotion or sponsorship rather than genuine editorial, artistic or academic content or genuine social or political commentary. This is obviously the case if an insertion is made for commercial, tobacco-related reasons, for example, paid placement of tobacco products or images in the media.

Recommendation
Implementation of a comprehensive ban on tobacco advertising, promotion and sponsorship need not interfere with legitimate types of expression, such as journalistic, artistic or academic expression or legitimate social or political commentary. Parties should, however, take measures to prevent the use of journalistic, artistic or academic expression or social or political commentary for the promotion of tobacco use or tobacco products.

Depictions of tobacco in entertainment media

The depiction of tobacco in entertainment media products, such as films, theatre and games, can strongly influence tobacco use, particularly among young people. Therefore, Parties should take the following measures:

- Implement a mechanism requiring that when an entertainment media product depicts tobacco products, use or imagery of any type, the responsible executives at each company involved in the production, distribution or presentation of that entertainment media product certify that no money, gifts, free publicity, interest-free loans, tobacco products, public relations assistance or anything else of any value has been given in exchange for the depiction.

- Prohibit the depiction of identifiable tobacco brands or tobacco brand images in association with, or as part of the content of, any entertainment media product.

- Require the display of prescribed anti-tobacco advertisements at the beginning of any entertainment media product that depicts tobacco products, use or images.

- Implement a ratings or classification system that takes into account the depiction of tobacco products, use or images in rating or classifying entertainment media products (for example, requiring adult ratings which restrict access of minors) and that ensures that entertainment media aimed at children (including cartoons) do not depict tobacco products, use or imagery.

Recommendation

Parties should take particular measures concerning the depiction of tobacco in entertainment media products, including requiring certification that no benefits have been received for any tobacco depictions, prohibiting the use of identifiable tobacco brands or imagery, requiring anti-tobacco advertisements and implementing a ratings or classification system that takes tobacco depictions into account.

Communication within the tobacco trade

The objective of banning tobacco advertising, promotion and sponsorship can usually be achieved without banning communications within the tobacco trade.

Any exception to a comprehensive ban on tobacco advertising, promotion and sponsorship for the purpose of providing product information to actors within the tobacco trade should be defined and applied strictly. Access to such information should be restricted to those persons who make trading decisions and who consequently need the information.

Tobacco manufacturers' newsletters can be exempted from the comprehensive ban on tobacco advertising, promotion and sponsorship, but only if they are destined exclusively for the manufacturer's employees, contractors, suppliers and other business partners and only to the extent that their distribution is limited to those persons or entities.

Recommendation

Any exception to a comprehensive ban on tobacco advertising, promotion and sponsorship to allow communication within the tobacco trade should be defined and applied strictly.

Constitutional principles in relation to a comprehensive ban

Any Party whose constitution or constitutional principles impose constraints on undertaking a comprehensive ban should, under Article 13 of the Convention, apply restrictions that are as comprehensive as possible in the light of those constraints. All Parties are obliged to undertake a comprehensive ban unless they are "not in a position" to do so "*due to* [their] constitution or constitutional principles". This obligation is to be interpreted in the context of the "recogni[tion] that a comprehensive ban on advertising, promotion and sponsorship would reduce the consumption of tobacco products", and in the light of the Convention's overall objective "to protect present and future generations from the devastating health, social, environmental and economic consequences of tobacco consumption and exposure to tobacco smoke" (Article 3 of the Convention).

It is acknowledged that the question of how constitutional principles are to be accommodated is to be determined by each Party's constitutional system.

Guidelines for implementation: Article 13

OBLIGATIONS RELATED TO ARTICLE 13.4 OF THE CONVENTION

Under Articles 13.2 and 13.3 of the Convention, Parties are obliged to undertake a comprehensive ban on tobacco advertising, promotion and sponsorship (or apply restrictions that are as comprehensive as possible in light of their constitution or constitutional principles). Some forms of tobacco advertising, promotion and sponsorship can be expected to persist in Parties that have not yet met their obligations under Articles 13.2 and 13.3 of the Convention. In addition, some very limited forms of relevant commercial communication, recommendation or action might continue to exist after a comprehensive ban has been implemented, and some forms of tobacco advertising, promotion and sponsorship may continue in Parties whose constitutions or constitutional principles prevent a comprehensive ban.

Any form of tobacco advertising, promotion or sponsorship that is not prohibited is obliged to meet the requirements of Article 13.4 of the Convention. Notably, these requirements include to "prohibit all forms of tobacco advertising, promotion and sponsorship that promote a tobacco product by any means that are false, misleading or deceptive or likely to create an erroneous impression about its characteristics, health effects, hazards or emissions" (13.4(a)); to "require that health or other appropriate warnings or messages accompany all tobacco advertising and, as appropriate, promotion and sponsorship" (13.4(b)); and to "require, if [a Party] does not have a comprehensive ban, the disclosure to relevant governmental authorities of expenditures by the tobacco industry on advertising, promotion and sponsorship not yet prohibited" (13.4(d)).

Parties should prohibit the use of any term, descriptor, trademark, emblem, marketing image, logo, colour and figurative or any other sign[7] that promotes a tobacco product or tobacco use, whether directly or indirectly, by any means that are false, misleading or deceptive or likely to create an erroneous impression about the characteristics, health effects, hazards or emissions of any tobacco product or tobacco products, or about the health effects or hazards of tobacco use. Such a prohibition should cover, inter alia, use of the terms "low tar", "light", "ultra-light", "mild", "extra", "ultra" and other terms in any language that may be misleading or create an erroneous impression.[8]

Parties should consider giving health or other warnings and messages accompanying any tobacco advertising, promotion and sponsorship at least equal prominence to the advertising, promotion or sponsorship. The content of the required warnings and messages should be prescribed by the relevant authorities and should effectively communicate the health risks and addictiveness of tobacco use, discourage the use of tobacco products and increase motivation to quit tobacco use. In order to maximize their effectiveness, the warnings or other messages required by Parties under

---

[7] These phrases are taken from Article 11.1(a) of the Convention, with the addition of the word "colour", which the working group recognizes can be used to convey a misleading impression about the characteristics, health effects or hazards of tobacco products.

[8] See Article 11.1(a) and the guidelines on Article 11 of the Convention.

Article 13.4(b) of the Convention should be consistent with the warnings or other messages on packaging that the Convention requires under Article 11.

Parties should require disclosure by the tobacco industry to relevant governmental authorities of any advertising, promotion and sponsorship in which it engages. The disclosures should be made at regular intervals prescribed by law and in response to specific requests. They should include, both in total and by brand, information about:

- the kind of advertising, promotion or sponsorship, including its content, form and type of media;
- the placement and extent or frequency of the advertising, promotion or sponsorship;
- the identity of all entities involved in the advertising, promotion and sponsorship, including advertising and production companies;
- in the case of cross-border advertising, promotion or sponsorship originating from a Party's territory, the territory or territories in which it is intended to be, or may be, received; and
- the amount of financial or other resources used for the advertising, promotion or sponsorship.

Parties should make the information readily available to the public (e.g. via the Internet)[9] while ensuring the protection of trade secrets.

While the obligations stated in Article 13.4(d) of the Convention regarding disclosure of expenditures by the tobacco industry on advertising, promotion and sponsorship that is not yet prohibited apply only to Parties that do not have a comprehensive ban, all Parties should implement the recommended measures in line with Article 13.5, which encourages Parties to implement measures beyond their obligations under Article 13.4. Requiring disclosure by the tobacco industry of expenditures on all advertising, promotion and sponsorship in which it engages may help Parties that consider that they have a comprehensive ban to identify any advertising, promotion or sponsorship not covered by the ban or engaged in by the tobacco industry in contravention of the ban. Disclosure requirements may have the added benefit of discouraging the tobacco industry from engaging in tobacco advertising, promotion or sponsorship in which it might otherwise engage.

Recommendation

Parties should meet the requirements of Article 13.4 of the Convention regarding any form of tobacco advertising, promotion or sponsorship that is not prohibited. Parties should prohibit all promotion of a tobacco product by any means that are false, misleading, deceptive or likely to create an erroneous impression; mandate health or other appropriate warnings or messages; and require regular disclosure by the tobacco industry to authorities of any advertising, promotion and sponsorship in which it engages. Parties should make the disclosed information readily available to the public.

---

[9] This provision supports the obligation under Article 12(c) to promote public access to a wide range of information on the tobacco industry as relevant to the objectives of the Convention.

CONSISTENCY

Domestic bans and their effective enforcement are the cornerstones of any meaningful comprehensive ban on tobacco advertising, promotion and sponsorship at the global level. Contemporary media platforms such as the Internet, films and direct broadcast satellite easily cross borders, and many forms of advertising, promotion and sponsorship regulated by domestic rules, such as event sponsorship, are broadcast and disseminated widely to other States. Moreover, advertising and promotion are often linked to products such as items of clothing and technological devices or appear in publications, and thus move from one State to another when these items move.

It is obvious that the effectiveness of domestic bans can be undermined unless there is international cooperation.

Cross-border advertising, promotion and sponsorship originating from a Party's territory (out-flowing material)

Article 13.2 of the Convention states that "a comprehensive ban shall include, subject to the legal environment and technical means available to [each] Party, a comprehensive ban on cross-border advertising, promotion and sponsorship *originating from its territory*".

Implementation of the ban should cover, for example, all publications and products printed or produced within the territory of a Party, whether they are targeting persons within the Party's territory or persons in the territories of other States. It is often difficult to differentiate between publications or products targeting or actually used in the originating State and those targeting and used in other States.

The ban should also apply to the placing of tobacco advertising, promotion and sponsorship on the Internet or another cross-border communications technology by any person or entity within the territory of a Party, whether the material is targeting persons outside or inside that Party's territory.

Moreover, the ban should also apply to any person or entity that broadcasts tobacco advertising, promotion and sponsorship that could be received in another State.

A comprehensive ban on advertising, promotion and sponsorship originating from a Party's territory should also ensure that a Party's nationals – natural persons or legal persons – do not engage in advertising, promotion or sponsorship in the territory of another State, irrespective of whether it is imported back to their State of origin.

Cross-border advertising, promotion and sponsorship entering a Party's territory

Article 13.7 of the Convention states that "Parties which have a ban on certain forms of tobacco advertising, promotion and sponsorship have the sovereign right to ban those forms of cross-border tobacco advertising, promotion and sponsorship entering their territory and to impose equal penalties as those applicable to domestic advertising, promotion and sponsorship originating from their territory in accordance with their national law".

Implementation of the ban should cover, for example, publications and products printed or produced in other States entering the territory of a Party or targeting persons in that territory. Parties should consider carrying out sampling checks for imported consignments of printed publications. If such publications are printed, published or distributed by nationals of a Party or by entities established in a Party's territory, they should be held liable and the ban should be enforced to the fullest extent possible.[10] The ban should also apply to all Internet content that is accessible within a Party's territory and to any other audio, visual or audiovisual material broadcast into or otherwise received in a Party's territory, whether or not it is targeting persons in the territory of that Party.

Recommendations

Parties with a comprehensive ban or restrictions on tobacco advertising, promotion and sponsorship should ensure that any cross-border tobacco advertising, promotion and sponsorship originating from their territory is banned or restricted in the same manner as domestic tobacco advertising, promotion and sponsorship. Parties should make use of their sovereign right to take effective actions to limit or prevent any cross-border tobacco advertising, promotion and sponsorship entering their territory, whether from Parties that have restrictions or from non-Parties, recognizing that in some cases effective actions might have to be addressed in a protocol.

RESPONSIBLE ENTITIES

The responsible entities should be defined widely, covering the entire marketing chain. Primary responsibility should lie with the initiator of advertising, promotion or sponsorship, usually tobacco manufacturers, wholesale distributors, importers, retailers and their agents and associations.

Moreover, many other entities are involved in tobacco advertising, promotion and sponsorship and should also be held responsible.

Responsibility cannot be attributed in the same manner to all entities as their involvement in the production, placement and dissemination of tobacco

---

[10] A Party may also enforce its ban against non-nationals in some circumstances. How to address nationals of other Parties may be the subject of provisions of a possible protocol on cross-border advertising, promotion and sponsorship.

advertising, promotion and sponsorship varies. In the case of tobacco sponsorship, the responsible entities are those that make any relevant form of contribution, those that receive any relevant form of contribution and any intermediaries that facilitate the making or receiving of any relevant form of contribution. When tobacco advertising and promotion involve communication, the way in which entities should be held responsible depends on their role in the production and dissemination of the content of the communication and the possibilities they have to control it. The disseminator should be made responsible in so far as it is aware of, or was in a position to become aware of, the content of the advertising and promotion. This is true for whatever media or communications technology is involved, but it applies especially to controlling content on the Internet and disseminated via direct broadcast satellite.

In relation to all forms of media and communications:

- Persons or entities that produce or publish content (e.g. advertising agencies, designers, publishers of newspapers and other printed materials, broadcasters and producers of films, television and radio programmes, games and live performances, and Internet, mobile phone, satellite and game content producers) should be banned from including tobacco advertising, promotion and sponsorship.
- Persons or entities such as media and events organizers, sportspeople, celebrities, film stars and other artists should be banned from engaging in tobacco advertising, promotion and sponsorship.
- Particular obligations (for example, remove or disable access to content) should be applied to other entities involved in analogue or digital media and communication (such as social networking sites, Internet service providers and telecommunication companies), once they have been made aware of tobacco advertising, promotion and sponsorship.

In the case of legal entities, the responsibility should normally lie with the company, not with an individual employee.

A contract, agreement or arrangement concerning tobacco advertising, promotion or sponsorship should be held invalid if it is agreed in violation of a comprehensive ban.

In relation to the Internet, for example, there are five principal categories of responsible entity upon which bans or particular obligations should be imposed.

- *Content producers* create the content or cause it to be created. These include tobacco companies, advertising agencies and producers of television programmes, films and games that are distributed online. Content producers should be *banned* from including tobacco advertising, promotion or sponsorship in the content they produce.

- *Content publishers* include publishers and entities that select content before it is made available to Internet users (e.g. Internet sites of newspapers or broadcasters). Content publishers should be *banned* from including tobacco advertising, promotion or sponsorship in the content they make available.
- *Content hosts* are entities that control Internet-connected computer servers on which content is stored, including entities that aggregate content produced by others without selecting the content before they make it available to Internet users (such as social networking Internet sites). Content hosts should have an *obligation to remove or disable access to* tobacco advertising, promotion and sponsorship *once they have been made aware of the content*.
- *Content navigators* are entities, such as Internet search engines, that facilitate the location of content by users of communications services. Content navigators should have an *obligation to disable access to* tobacco advertising, promotion and sponsorship *once they have been made aware of the content*.
- *Access providers* are entities that provide end-user access to communications services, such as Internet service providers and mobile telephone companies. Access providers should have an *obligation to disable access to* tobacco advertising, promotion and sponsorship *once they have been made aware of the content*.

Unlike the obligations on content producers, content publishers and content hosts, Parties could limit the obligations on content navigators and access providers to using reasonable efforts to disable access in light of what is technically possible.

Recommendation

The entities responsible for tobacco advertising, promotion and sponsorship should be defined widely, and the way in which they are held responsible should depend on their role.

Primary responsibility should lie with the initiator of advertising, promotion or sponsorship, usually tobacco manufacturers, wholesale distributors, importers, retailers and their agents and associations.

Persons or entities that produce or publish media content should be banned from including tobacco advertising, promotion and sponsorship in the content they produce or publish.

Persons or entities (such as events organizers, sportspeople and celebrities) should be banned from engaging in tobacco advertising, promotion and sponsorship.

Particular obligations, for example, to remove content should be applied to other entities involved in analogue or digital media after they have been made aware of the tobacco advertising, promotion and sponsorship.

DOMESTIC ENFORCEMENT OF LAWS ON TOBACCO ADVERTISING, PROMOTION AND SPONSORSHIP

Sanctions

Parties should introduce and apply effective, proportionate and dissuasive penalties (including fines, corrective advertising remedies and licence suspension or cancellation). In order that the penalties imposed be effective deterrents they should be graded and commensurate with the nature and seriousness of the offence(s), including a first offence, and should outweigh the potential economic benefits to be derived from the advertising, promotion or sponsorship.

Repeat infringements should incur a highly significant penalty for a manufacturer or responsible entity. In the case of frequent or flagrant infringements, more stringent sanctions should be imposed, including possible imprisonment. Sanctions should also include the obligation to remedy the infringement, for example by:

- removal of the advertising, promotion or sponsorship;
- publication of court decisions in a manner to be determined by the court and at the expense of the party or parties designated by the court; and
- funding of corrective or counter-advertising.

Sanctions should be applied to the conduct of entities and not only to individuals (including corporate entities that can be held responsible for the conduct of related corporate entities outside the territory but with an effect within the territory). Sanctions should also be applied to the conduct of managers, directors, officers and/or legal representatives of corporate entities when those individuals bear responsibility for the corporate entity's conduct.

Licensing of tobacco manufacturers, wholesale distributors, importers and retailers can be an effective method for controlling advertising, promotion and sponsorship. A licence would be granted or renewed only if the applicant could ensure compliance with the legal requirements. In cases of non-compliance, the licence could be withdrawn for a certain time or cancelled. For responsible entities not directly involved in producing or selling tobacco (such as broadcasters) when such entities are required to be licensed, compliance with the provisions on tobacco advertising, promotion and sponsorship should be included in the criteria for granting, renewing, suspending or revoking a licence.

If deterrent sanctions are in place, enforcement authorities might be successful in putting an end to illegal practices without court proceedings (e.g. by contacts, meetings, warnings, administrative decisions and periodic penalty payments).

Monitoring, enforcement and access to justice

Parties should designate a competent, independent authority to monitor and enforce the laws and entrust it with the necessary powers and resources. This agency should have the power to investigate complaints, seize unlawful advertising or promotion, and pronounce on complaints and/or initiate appropriate legal proceedings.

Civil society and citizens should be involved in the monitoring and effective enforcement of the ban. Civil society organizations, notably entities such as public health, health care, prevention, youth protection or consumer organizations, can be expected to undertake rigorous monitoring, and legislation should specify that members of the public may initiate complaints.

In addition, civil law options should be made available to oppose tobacco advertising, promotion and sponsorship. National law should enable any interested person or nongovernmental organization to initiate legal action against illegal tobacco advertising, promotion and sponsorship.

The enforcement programme may include a toll-free telephone complaint hotline, an Internet web site or a similar system to encourage the public to report violations.

Recommendation

Parties should introduce and apply effective, proportionate and dissuasive penalties. Parties should designate a competent, independent authority to monitor and enforce the law and entrust it with the necessary powers and resources. Civil society should be involved in the monitoring and enforcement of the law and have access to justice.

PUBLIC EDUCATION AND COMMUNITY AWARENESS

In the spirit of Article 12 of the Convention,[11] Parties should promote and strengthen public awareness of tobacco advertising, promotion and sponsorship in all sectors of society, using all available communication tools. Parties should, inter alia, adopt appropriate measures to promote broad access to effective, comprehensive public education and awareness programmes that underline the importance of a comprehensive ban, educate the public concerning its necessity and explain why advertising, promotion and sponsorship by the tobacco industry is unacceptable.

Engaging the support of the community to monitor compliance and report violations of laws against tobacco advertising, promotion and sponsorship is an essential element of enforcement. In order for members of the community to perform this role, they must be made aware of the problem and understand the law and the ways in which they can act on breaches.

---

[11] "Education, communication, training and public awareness".

Parties should implement public education and awareness programmes, inform members of the community about existing laws on tobacco advertising, promotion and sponsorship, the steps that can be taken to inform the relevant government agency of any advertising, promotion or sponsorship, and the steps that can be taken against a person who has engaged in tobacco advertising, promotion or sponsorship in breach of the law.

Recommendation

Parties should promote and strengthen, in all sectors of society, public awareness of the need to eliminate tobacco advertising, promotion and sponsorship, the laws against it, and the ways in which members of the public can act on breaches of these laws.

INTERNATIONAL COLLABORATION

The effectiveness of efforts to eliminate tobacco advertising, promotion and sponsorship depends not only on the initiatives undertaken by individual Parties but also on the extent to which Parties cooperate in addressing tobacco advertising, promotion and sponsorship. Effective international cooperation will be essential to the elimination of both domestic and cross-border tobacco advertising, promotion and sponsorship.

Parties to the Convention already have undertaken commitments with respect to international cooperation, including under Article 13.6 (*Cooperation in the development of technologies and other means necessary to facilitate the elimination of cross-border advertising*); Article 19 (*Liability*); Article 20 (*Research, surveillance and exchange of information*); particularly Article 20.4 (*Exchange of publicly available, scientific, technical, socioeconomic, commercial and legal information, as well as information regarding the practices of the tobacco industry*); Article 21 (*Reporting and exchange of information*); Article 22 (*Cooperation in the scientific, technical, and legal fields and provision of related expertise*); and Article 26 (*Financial resources*).

In addition to the recommendations in these guidelines, the Conference of the Parties also takes note of the recommendations of the working group on other measures with respect to facilitation of the exchange of information and other cooperation between Parties that would contribute to the elimination of cross-border advertising, promotion and sponsorship.[12] Such measures to eliminate domestic tobacco advertising, promotion or sponsorship are also beneficial, recognizing that Parties would benefit from sharing information, experience and expertise in respect of *all* tobacco advertising, promotion and sponsorship, not only cross-border tobacco advertising, promotion and sponsorship.

---

[12] Decision FCTC/COP3(14)

APPENDIX

Indicative (non-exhaustive) list of forms of tobacco advertising, promotion and sponsorship within the terms of the Convention

- communication through audio, visual or audiovisual means: print (including newspapers, magazines, pamphlets, leaflets, flyers, letters, billboards, posters, signs), television and radio (including terrestrial and satellite), films, DVDs, videos and CDs, games (computer games, video games or online games), other digital communication platforms (including the Internet and mobile phones) and theatre or other live performance;
- brand-marking, including in entertainment venues and retail outlets and on vehicles and equipment (e.g. by use of brand colours or schemes of colours, logos or trademarks);
- display of tobacco products at points of sale;
- tobacco product vending machines;
- Internet sales of tobacco products;
- brand stretching and brand sharing (product diversification);
- product placement (i.e. the inclusion of, or reference to, a tobacco product, service or trademark in the context of communication (see above), in return for payment or other consideration);
- provision of gifts or discounted products with the purchase of tobacco products (e.g. key rings, T-shirts, baseball hats, cigarette lighters);
- supply of free samples of tobacco products, including in conjunction with marketing surveys and taste testing;
- incentive promotions or loyalty schemes, e.g. redeemable coupons provided with purchase of tobacco products;
- competitions, associated with tobacco products or brand names, whether requiring the purchase of a tobacco product or not;
- direct targeting of individuals with promotional (including informational) material, such as direct mail, telemarketing, "consumer surveys" or "research";
- promotion of discounted products;
- sale or supply of toys or sweets that resemble tobacco products;
- payments or other contributions to retailers to encourage or induce them to sell products, including retailer incentive programmes (e.g. rewards to retailers for achieving certain sales volumes);
- packaging and product design features;
- payment or other consideration in exchange for the exclusive sale or prominent display of a particular product or particular manufacturer's product in a retail outlet, at a venue or at an event;
- sale, supply, placement and display of products at educational establishments or at hospitality, sporting, entertainment, music, dance and social venues or events;

provision of financial or other support to events, activities, individuals or groups (such as sporting or arts events, individual sportspeople or teams, individual artists or artistic groups, welfare organizations, politicians, political candidates or political parties), whether or not in exchange for publicity, including corporate social responsibility activities; and

provision of financial or other support by the tobacco industry to venue operators (such as pubs, clubs or other recreational venues) in exchange for building or renovating premises to promote tobacco products or the use or provision of awnings and sunshades.

Guidelines for implementation
Article 14

Guidelines for implementation of Article 14 of the WHO Framework Convention on Tobacco Control

DEMAND REDUCTION MEASURES CONCERNING TOBACCO DEPENDENCE AND CESSATION

INTRODUCTION

Article 14 of the WHO Framework Convention on Tobacco Control (WHO FCTC) states that "each Party shall develop and disseminate appropriate, comprehensive and integrated guidelines based on scientific evidence and best practices, taking into account national circumstances and priorities, and shall take effective measures to promote cessation of tobacco use and adequate treatment for tobacco dependence".

Tobacco dependence treatment is defined differently by different cultures and in different languages. It sometimes includes measures to reduce tobacco use in the population as a whole, but often only refers to interventions at the individual level. These guidelines cover both, and therefore employ the term "promotion of tobacco cessation" as well as "tobacco dependence treatment". Further effective measures to promote cessation of tobacco use are contained in other articles of the WHO FCTC and in the guidelines on their implementation.

Parties are encouraged to use these guidelines to assist them in fulfilling their obligations under the WHO FCTC and in protecting public health. They are also encouraged to implement measures beyond those recommended by the guidelines, in accordance with the provisions of Article 2.1 of the Convention.[1]

Purpose

The purpose of these guidelines is to assist Parties in meeting their obligations under Article 14 of the WHO FCTC, consistent with their obligations under other provisions of the Convention and with the intentions of the Conference of the Parties, on the basis of the best available scientific evidence and taking into account national circumstances and priorities.

To this end the guidelines:

    (i) encourage Parties to strengthen or create a sustainable infrastructure which motivates attempts to quit, ensures wide

---

[1] Parties are directed to the WHO FCTC web site (http://www.who.int/fctc/) where further sources of information on topics covered by these guidelines are maintained.

access to support for tobacco users who wish to quit, and provides sustainable resources to ensure that such support is available;

(ii) identify the key, effective measures needed to promote tobacco cessation and incorporate tobacco dependence treatment into national tobacco control programmes and health-care systems;

(iii) urge Parties to share experiences and collaborate in order to facilitate the development or strengthening of support for tobacco cessation and tobacco dependence treatment.

Use of terms

For the purpose of these guidelines, the following definitions apply:

- "Tobacco user": a person who uses any tobacco product.
- "Tobacco addiction/dependence": a cluster of behavioural, cognitive, and physiological phenomena that develop after repeated tobacco use and that typically include a strong desire to use tobacco, difficulties in controlling its use, persistence in tobacco use despite harmful consequences, a higher priority given to tobacco use than to other activities and obligations, increased tolerance, and sometimes a physical withdrawal state.[2]
- "Tobacco cessation": the process of stopping the use of any tobacco product, with or without assistance.
- "Promotion of tobacco cessation": population-wide measures and approaches that contribute to stopping tobacco use, including tobacco dependence treatment.
- "Tobacco dependence treatment": the provision of behavioural support or medications, or both, to tobacco users, to help them stop their tobacco use.[3]
- "Behavioural support": support, other than medications, aimed at helping people stop their tobacco use. It can include all cessation assistance that imparts knowledge about tobacco use and quitting, provides support and teaches skills and strategies for changing behaviour.
- "Brief advice": advice to stop using tobacco, usually taking only a few minutes, given to all tobacco users, usually during the course of a routine consultation or interaction.

---

[2] Definition adapted from: *International statistical classification of diseases and related health problems,* tenth revision (ICD–10). Geneva, World Health Organization, 2007.
[3] Sometimes called "cessation support" in this document.

UNDERLYING CONSIDERATIONS

Tobacco use is highly addictive.[4,5] The use of tobacco and exposure to tobacco smoke have severe negative health, economic, environmental and social consequences, and people should be educated about these negative consequences and the benefits of cessation.[6] Knowledge of these negative consequences is a powerful component of most tobacco users' motivation to quit, and therefore it is important to ensure that they are fully understood by the public and policy-makers.

It is important to implement tobacco dependence treatment measures synergistically with other tobacco control measures. The promotion of tobacco cessation and treatment of tobacco dependence are key components of a comprehensive, integrated tobacco control programme. Support for tobacco users in their cessation efforts and successful treatment of their tobacco dependence will reinforce other tobacco control policies, by increasing social support for them and increasing their acceptability. Implementing cessation and treatment measures in conjunction with population level interventions covered by other articles of the WHO FCTC, will have a synergistic effect and thus maximize their impact.

Tobacco cessation and tobacco dependence treatment strategies should be based on the best available evidence of effectiveness. There is clear scientific evidence that tobacco dependence treatment is effective and that it is a cost-effective health-care intervention, and thus that it is a worthwhile investment for health-care systems.

Treatment should be accessible and affordable. Tobacco dependence treatment should be widely available, accessible and affordable, and should include education[7] on the range of cessation options available.

Tobacco cessation and tobacco dependence treatment should be inclusive. Tobacco cessation strategies and tobacco dependence treatment should take into account factors such as gender, culture, religion, age, educational background, literacy, socioeconomic status, disability, and the needs of groups with high rates of tobacco use. Tobacco cessation strategies should be as inclusive as possible, and should where appropriate be tailored to the needs of individual tobacco users.

Monitoring and evaluation are essential. Monitoring and evaluation are essential components of successful tobacco cessation and tobacco dependence treatment programmes.

Active partnership with civil society. The active participation of and partnership with civil society, as specified in the Preamble and in Article 4.7 of the WHO FCTC, are essential to the effective implementation of these guidelines.

---

[4] See *International statistical classification of diseases and related health problems,* tenth revision (ICD–10). Geneva, World Health Organization, 2007.
[5] The terms addiction and dependence are used interchangeably in these guidelines, as in the Preamble and Articles 4 and 5 of the WHO FCTC.
[6] As outlined in Article 12 of the WHO FCTC.
[7] Further guidance on education is given in the guidelines on implementation of Article 12 of the WHO FCTC adopted in decision FCTC/COP/4(7).

Protection from all commercial and vested interests. Development of strategies to implement Article 14 of the WHO FCTC should be protected from the commercial and other vested interests of the tobacco industry, in line with Article 5.3 of the Convention and its guidelines, and from all other actual and potential conflicts of interest.

Value of sharing experience. Sharing of experience and collaboration with each other will greatly enhance Parties' abilities to implement these guidelines.

Central role of health-care systems. Strengthening existing health-care systems to promote tobacco cessation and tobacco dependence treatment is essential.

DEVELOPING AN INFRASTRUCTURE TO SUPPORT TOBACCO CESSATION AND TREATMENT OF TOBACCO DEPENDENCE

Background

Certain infrastructure elements will be needed to promote tobacco cessation and provide effective tobacco dependence treatment. Much of this infrastructure (such as a primary health care system) already exists in many countries. In order to promote tobacco cessation and develop tobacco dependence treatment as rapidly as possible and at as low a cost as possible, Parties should use existing resources and infrastructure as much as they can, and ensure that tobacco users at least receive brief advice. Once this has been achieved, other mechanisms for providing tobacco dependence treatment, including more specialist approaches (see "Developing cessation support: a stepwise approach" below), can be put in place.

Professional associations and other groups with relevant expertise in this area should be involved at an early stage in the design and development of the necessary infrastructure, but with the process protected from all actual and potential conflicts of interest.

Recommendation

Parties should implement the actions listed below in order to strengthen or create the infrastructure needed to promote cessation of tobacco use effectively and provide adequate treatment for tobacco dependence, taking into account national circumstances and priorities.

Actions

Conduct a national situation analysis

Analyse, where appropriate: (1) the status of all tobacco control policies in the country and their impact, especially in motivating tobacco users to quit and creating demand for treatment support; (2) policies to promote tobacco cessation and provide tobacco dependence treatment; (3) existing tobacco dependence treatment services and their impact; (4) the resources available to strengthen the promotion of tobacco cessation and tobacco dependence treatment services (or to create such services where they do not yet exist), including training capacity,[8] health-care infrastructure, and any other infrastructure that may be helpful; (5) any monitoring data available (see "Monitoring and evaluation" below). Use this situation analysis where appropriate to create a strategic plan.

Create or strengthen national coordination

Ensure that the national coordinating mechanism or focal point facilitates the strengthening or creation of a programme to promote tobacco cessation and provide tobacco dependence treatment.

Maintain or consider creating an up-to-date, easily accessible information system on available tobacco cessation services and qualified service providers for tobacco users.

Develop and disseminate comprehensive guidelines

Parties should develop and disseminate comprehensive tobacco dependence treatment guidelines based on the best available scientific evidence and best practices, taking into account national circumstances and priorities. These guidelines should include two major components: (1) a **national cessation strategy**, to promote tobacco cessation and provide tobacco dependence treatment, aimed principally at those responsible for funding and implementing policies and programmes; and (2) **national treatment guidelines**[9] aimed principally at those who will develop, manage and provide cessation support to tobacco users.

A national cessation strategy and national tobacco dependence treatment guidelines should have the following key characteristics:

- they should be evidence based;
- their development should be protected from all actual and potential conflicts of interest;
- they should be developed in collaboration with key stakeholders, including but not limited to health scientists, health professional organizations, health-care workers, educators, youth workers and nongovernmental organizations with relevant expertise in this area;
- they should be commissioned or led by government, but in active partnership and consultation with other stakeholders; however, if other organizations initiate the treatment guidelines development process, they should do so in active collaboration with government;
- they should include a dissemination and implementation plan, should highlight the importance of all service providers (within or outside the health-care sector) setting an example by not using tobacco,

---

[8] Further guidance on training is given in the guidelines on implementation of Article 12 of the WHO FCTC adopted in decision FCTC/COP4(7).
[9] Treatment guidelines are systematically developed statements to help service managers, practitioners and patients to make decisions about appropriate treatment for tobacco dependence and cessation.

and should be periodically reviewed and updated, in the light of developing scientific evidence, and in accordance with the obligations established by Article 5.1 of the WHO FCTC.

Additional key characteristics of national treatment guidelines:

- they should be widely endorsed at national level, including by health professional organizations and/or associations;
- they should include as broad a range of interventions as possible, such as systematic identification of people who use tobacco, provision of brief advice, quitlines, face-to-face behavioural support provided by workers trained to deliver it, systems to make medications accessible and free or at an affordable cost, and systems to support the key steps involved in helping people to quit tobacco use, including reporting tobacco use status in all medical notes;
- they should cover all settings and all providers, both within and outside the health-care sector.

Address tobacco use by health-care workers and others involved in tobacco cessation

Health-care workers should avoid using tobacco because:

- they are role models and by using tobacco they undermine public health messages about its effects on health;
- it is important to reduce the social acceptability of tobacco use and health-care workers have a particular responsibility to set a good example in this respect.

Specific programmes promoting cessation of tobacco use and offering tobacco dependence treatment should therefore be provided for health-care workers and any other groups involved in helping tobacco users to quit.

Develop training capacity[10]

In most countries the health-care system[11] and health-care workers should play a central role in promoting tobacco cessation and offering support to tobacco users who want to quit. However other groups should be involved where appropriate.

All health-care workers should be trained to record tobacco use, give brief advice, encourage a quit attempt, and refer tobacco users to specialized tobacco dependence treatment services where appropriate.

Outside health-care settings, other individuals can be trained to give brief advice, encourage a quit attempt, and refer tobacco users to specialized

---

[10] Further guidance on training is given in the guidelines on implementation of Article 12 of the WHO FCTC adopted in decision FCTC/COP4(7)

[11] Including but not limited to governmental bodies, public and private health-care facilities, and funding organizations.

tobacco dependence treatment services where appropriate, and therefore also have a role to play in tobacco cessation and tobacco dependence treatment.

Both health-care workers and those outside health-care settings who deliver intensive specialized support (see "Key components of a system to help tobacco users to quit" below) should be trained to the highest possible standard and receive continuous education.

Tobacco control and tobacco cessation should be incorporated into the training curricula of all health professionals and other relevant occupations both at pre- and post-qualification levels, and in continuous professional development. Training should include information about tobacco use and the harm it does, the benefits of cessation, and the influence that trained workers can have in prompting quitting.

Training standards should be set nationally by competent authorities.

Use existing systems and resources to ensure the greatest possible access to services

Parties should use existing infrastructure, in both health-care and other settings, to ensure that all tobacco users are identified and provided with at least brief advice.

Parties should use existing infrastructure to provide tobacco dependence treatment for people who want to stop using tobacco. Such treatment should be widely accessible, evidence based, and affordable.

Parties should consider using existing infrastructure that would provide the greatest possible access for tobacco users, including but not limited to primary health care and other services such as those providing treatment for tuberculosis and HIV/AIDS.

Make the recording of tobacco use in medical notes mandatory

Parties should ensure that the recording of tobacco use status in all medical and other relevant notes is mandatory, and should encourage the recording of tobacco use in death certification.

Encourage collaborative working

It is essential that governmental and nongovernmental organizations work in partnership, in accordance with the spirit of the underlying considerations of these guidelines, in order to make rapid progress in implementing the provisions of Article 14 of the WHO FCTC.

Establish a sustainable source of funding for cessation help

The strengthening or creation of a national infrastructure to promote tobacco cessation and to provide tobacco dependence treatment will require both financial and technical resources and it will therefore be essential to identify funding for that infrastructure, in accordance with Article 26 of the WHO FCTC.

In order to alleviate governmental budgetary pressure, Parties could consider placing the cost of cessation support on the tobacco industry and retailers, through such measures as: designated tobacco taxes; tobacco manufacturing and/or importing licensing fees; tobacco product registration fees; tobacco selling licenses for distributors and retailers; noncompliance fees levied on the tobacco industry and retailers, such as administrative monetary penalties; and annual tobacco surveillance/control fees for the tobacco industry and retailers. Successful action to reduce the illicit trade in tobacco products (as outlined in Article 15 of the WHO FCTC) could also increase government revenue substantially.

KEY COMPONENTS OF A SYSTEM TO HELP TOBACCO USERS QUIT

Background

Support can be offered to tobacco users in a wide variety of settings and by a wide variety of providers, as described in the previous section, and can include a range of options, from less intensive population-wide approaches to more intensive approaches delivered by specialists who are trained and may be paid. The key components of a system to help tobacco users quit include approaches with a wide reach like brief advice and quitlines[12] more intensive approaches like behavioural support delivered by trained specialists, and effective medications. There is a substantial body of scientific evidence showing that behavioural support and medications are effective and cost-effective, separately and combined, and that they are more effective when combined.

Recommendations

In designing national cessation and treatment systems for health-care and other settings, Parties should include the components listed below, taking into account national circumstances and priorities.

Parties should provide cessation support and treatment in all health-care settings and by all health-care providers. Parties should additionally consider providing cessation support and treatment in non-health-care settings and by suitably trained non-health-care providers, especially where scientific evidence suggests that some populations of tobacco users[13] may be better served in this way.

---

[12] A quitline is a telephone counselling service that can provide both reactive and proactive counselling. A reactive quitline provides an immediate response to a call initiated by the tobacco user, but only responds to incoming calls. A proactive quitline involves setting up a schedule of planned calls to tobacco users.
[13] Such populations may include, but not be limited to, young people, parents, and people of low socioeconomic status.

Actions

Establish population-level approaches

Mass communication. Mass communication and education programmes are essential for encouraging tobacco cessation, promoting support for tobacco cessation, and encouraging tobacco users to draw on this support.[14] These programmes can include both unpaid and paid media placements.

Brief advice. Brief advice should be integrated into all health-care systems. All health-care workers should be trained to ask about tobacco use, record it in the notes, give brief advice on stopping, and direct tobacco users to the most appropriate and effective treatment available locally. Brief advice should be implemented as an essential part of standard practice and its implementation should be monitored regularly.

Quitlines. All Parties should offer quitlines in which callers can receive advice from trained cessation specialists. Ideally they should be free and offer proactive support. Quitlines should be widely publicized and advertised, and adequately staffed, to ensure that tobacco users can always receive individual support. Parties are encouraged to include the quitline number on tobacco product packaging.

Establish more intensive individual approaches

Specialized tobacco dependence treatment services. Tobacco users who need cessation support should, where resources allow, be offered intensive specialized support, delivered by specially trained practitioners. Such services should offer behavioural support, and where appropriate, medications or advice on the provision of medications. The services may be delivered by a variety of health-care or other trained workers, including doctors, nurses, midwives, pharmacists, psychologists, and others, according to national circumstances. These services can be delivered in a wide variety of settings and should be easily accessible to tobacco users. Where possible they should be provided free or at an affordable cost. Specialized treatment services should meet national or applicable standards of care.

Make medications available

Medications that have been clearly shown by scientific evidence to increase the chances of tobacco cessation should be made available to tobacco users wanting to quit and where possible be provided free or at an affordable cost.

Some medications can also be made available population wide, with fewer restrictions to access, taking into account relevant legislation. Experience in some countries has shown that increasing the accessibility and availability of some medications can increase the number of attempts to quit.

Collective bargaining by governments or regional economic organizations should be used to reduce medication prices by bulk purchase or other available

---

[14] See the guidelines on implementation of Article 12 of the WHO FCTC adopted in decision FCTC/COP4(7).

means, to ensure that cessation treatment does not impose excessive costs on those stopping tobacco use. Where low-cost, effective[15] medications exist, these may be considered as a standard treatment.

Consider emerging research evidence and novel approaches and media

Parties should keep under review the developing scientific evidence of new approaches to promoting tobacco cessation and providing tobacco dependence treatment.

Parties should be open to new and innovative approaches to promoting tobacco cessation and providing tobacco dependence treatment, while at the same time prioritizing approaches that are more strongly based on the scientific evidence.

There is evidence from some countries that national No Smoking Days, sometimes held on World No Tobacco Day, can be effective low-cost interventions that motivate tobacco users to try to quit. Cellphone text messaging and Internet-based behavioural support may be especially useful in countries where telephone and Internet use are high. These and other approaches are being investigated in scientific trials, although there is insufficient evidence yet to recommend them as a core part of treatment provision. The potential of using electronic media like radio for delivering cessation messages and advice could also be explored, as in many countries radio is the most widespread and low-cost medium of mass communication. Some countries also have local and folk media which have wide access at the grass-roots level, and the use of these for disseminating information about availability of tobacco cessation facilities may be considered along with other culturally acceptable approaches to treatment.

DEVELOPING CESSATION SUPPORT: A STEPWISE APPROACH

Background

Tobacco control policies which reduce the demand for tobacco, and which are covered in other articles of the WHO FCTC,[16] promote tobacco cessation by encouraging quitting and creating a supportive environment for the implementation of measures that support cessation. Implementing tobacco cessation and tobacco dependence treatment measures in conjunction with such policies will have a synergistic effect and thus maximize the impact on public health.

Even a country with a low proportion of tobacco users wanting to quit and needing help to do so may have large demand for cessation support, if the absolute number of tobacco users is high.

Introduction of the different components of a comprehensive, integrated system to promote tobacco cessation and treat tobacco dependence can

---

[15] According to the scientific evidence (see "Monitoring and evaluation" below).
[16] Including, but not limited to, Articles 6, 8, 11, 12 and 13.

be simultaneous or stepwise, according to each Party's circumstances and priorities. Some Parties already have comprehensive treatment systems, and all Parties should aim to provide the fullest complement of interventions for tobacco cessation and treatment of tobacco dependence.

Resources are finite however, so this section suggests the elements of a stepwise approach to developing tobacco dependence treatment, if such an approach is deemed appropriate.

Recommendations

Parties that have not already done so should implement measures to promote tobacco cessation and increase demand for tobacco dependence treatment contained in other articles of the WHO FCTC.[17]

Parties should use existing infrastructure, in both health-care and other settings, to ensure that all tobacco users are identified and provided with at least brief advice.

Parties should implement the actions listed below, taking into account national circumstances and priorities.

Actions

>   Actions that establish basic infrastructure and create an environment that prompts quit attempts

Establish system components
- Ensure that the population is well informed about the harmful effects of tobacco products.
- Strengthen or create – and fund – national coordination for tobacco cessation and tobacco dependence treatment, as part of the national tobacco control plan.
- Develop and disseminate a national tobacco cessation strategy and national tobacco dependence treatment guidelines.
- Identify and allocate sustainable funding for tobacco cessation and tobacco dependence treatment programmes.
- Where appropriate, ensure that health insurance or other funded health-care systems record tobacco dependence as a disease or disorder and include its treatment in services covered.

---

[17] Including, but not limited to, Articles 6, 8, 11, 12 and 13.

Address the issue in health-care workers

- Incorporate tobacco dependence and cessation into the core curriculum and continuing professional training of medical, dental, nursing, pharmacy and other relevant undergraduate and postgraduate courses and in licensing and certifying examinations.
- Train health-care workers to give brief advice according to a simple formula.
- Where appropriate train workers and service providers outside the health-care sector in tobacco cessation and tobacco dependence treatment skills.
- Promote tobacco cessation among health-care workers and service providers who use tobacco, and offer support to them to quit if they need it.

Integrate brief advice into existing health-care systems

- Ensure that tobacco use is recorded in medical notes and other relevant notes at all levels of care.
- Integrate brief advice into the existing primary health-care system.
- Involve all relevant sectors of a country's health-care system in providing brief advice.
- Integrate brief advice into other culturally relevant settings outside the health-care sector when the opportunity or necessity arises.
- Reimbursement of health-care workers' time for tobacco cessation counselling, and of the costs of medications, is recommended where appropriate.

Actions that increase the likelihood of quit attempts succeeding

Create capacity for tobacco cessation support and tobacco dependence treatment

- Ensure that the population is well informed about the availability and accessibility of tobacco dependence treatment services and encourage them to make use of them.
- Establish a free proactive quitline providing advice on how to quit, or if resources are scarce, start by establishing a free reactive quitline.
- Ensure that effective medications are readily available, accessible, and free or at an affordable cost.
- Establish a network of specialized comprehensive tobacco dependence treatment services that meet national or applicable standards of care.

MONITORING AND EVALUATION

Background

Monitoring and evaluation activities measure the progress and impact of an intervention or programme by collecting data/information showing change, or the lack of it. This includes periodically reviewing interventions and programmes. Scientific evidence is evidence gained by scientific enquiry, usually through formal research, and includes evidence obtained through monitoring and evaluation.[18]

Monitoring and evaluation are essential to ensure that the best means are employed to develop and deliver effective treatment to tobacco users. At national level, monitoring and evaluation ensure that progress is measured, so that interventions can be modified and improved as necessary, helping to ensure that the most efficient use is made of limited resources. Internationally, the sharing of experience will help Parties to adapt and improve their strategies.

There are national and international data collection systems that can be used to inform and support the collection of monitoring and evaluation data.

Recommendation

Parties should monitor and evaluate all tobacco cessation and tobacco dependence treatment strategies and programmes, including process and outcome measures, to observe trends. They should benefit from the experience of other countries through the exchange of information, in accordance with the provisions of Articles 20, 21 and 22 of the WHO FCTC.

Actions

Formulate measurable objectives, determine the resources required, and identify indicators to enable the assessment of progress towards each objective.

Encourage health-care workers and service providers to participate in the monitoring of service performance through clearly defined indicators, taking account of national circumstances and priorities.

Use data collection systems that are practical and efficient, built on strong methodologies, and are appropriate to local circumstances.

INTERNATIONAL COOPERATION

Background

International cooperation between Parties is a treaty obligation under Article 22 of the WHO FCTC. International cooperation in tobacco cessation and tobacco dependence treatment is also a means of supporting and strengthening the implementation of the Convention.

---

[18] See the guidelines on implementation of Article 12 of the WHO FCTC adopted in decision FCTC/COP4(7), for a definition of research-based evidence.

Recommendation

Parties should collaborate at the international level to ensure that they are able to implement the most effective measures for tobacco cessation, in accordance with the provisions of Articles 20, 21 and 22 of the WHO FCTC.

Actions

Share tobacco cessation and treatment experiences with other Parties, including strategies to develop and fund support for cessation of tobacco use, national treatment guidelines, training strategies, and data and reports from evaluations of tobacco dependence treatment systems.

Where appropriate, use international reporting mechanisms, such as regular reporting on the implementation of the WHO FCTC, and take advantage of bilateral and multilateral contacts and agreements.

Review and revise these guidelines periodically to ensure that they continue to provide effective guidance and assistance to Parties.